# USE IT - OR - LOSE IT
## The Word of Faith

by
ROY H. HICKS, D.D.

**HARRISON HOUSE**
**BOX 35035**
**TULSA, OK. 74135**

ISBN   0-89274-002-7

# TABLE OF CONTENTS

# PREFACE

"Use It — Or Lose It" may be a catchy phrase but, catchy as it may seem, it has a depth of meaning when applied to faith. The intent of this book is to reveal the great truth that "faith is a gift from God." This gift, if not used, will be lost . . . because unused, unapplied faith fast gives way to unbelief.

Most of God's laws, especially those in nature, teach that anything dammed up becomes unusable.

Our faith, God's gift, must flow out of our soul and spirit through our lips into positive action that will let all know that "we believe in God." Unused faith will become rusty if left alone and, when buffeted by the storms of life, will be too weak to prevail. However, if we use our gift of faith constantly in praise and in verbal expression, it will not only meet the challenge of life . . . but will increase.

The author has found that this book has been used by the Holy Spirit to heal many readers. Many were encouraged and have testified that these truths have revolutionized their lives.

Some may find they will need to read it several times to gain a clear picture. I pray the Holy Spirit will bring together in your life these thoughts, and His eternal word will flow from you because it has become part of your life.

# INTRODUCTION

Faith is always relevant. The New Testament Faith, the answer to all generations, is always contemporary. We hear the dissident voice of a new generation. Will this voice cause us to compromise eternal verities? Or will it stir within us a greater dedication to the *Faith* of our fathers? We believe in God with a faith that meets every cry of the human heart. It is, and always has been, the answer to every need of every generation.

Is the faith that was once delivered to the saints in jeopardy? This miraculous faith that the early church received was entrusted to the believer. The spirit-filled believer became the custodian of the faith. *It was never the intention of the Lord that the recipient become an expert in the realm of the moving of the spirit but remain a novice in the realm of faith.* The two are to work hand in hand.

When one announces that his topic is going to be faith, the reaction from some is a presumptive conclusion. A conclusion that the subject will be divine healing! While it is true that most of our immediate needs are those in the material, physical realm, it is not true that this is the realm of the most important and vital issues to us all. The immediate needs and our failure to meet them sometimes discourages us from pursuing the more essential things of God. These matters, of course, involve our faith. It is also true that some of the better illustrations concerning faith come to us by equating the immediate needs in the material and physical with faith and the spiritual realm.

We are always facing the almost hopeless task of taking the eternal things of an omnipotent God and making them simple and relevant to everyday life. Thus we have no choice but to deal primarily in the realm in which we are all most familiar and which we more easily understand. However, may we be very quick to point out that as far as the Kingdom of God is concerned, one has an almost impossible assignment of separating what is the most important. If a servant or saint of God is discouraged in either realm, he may be defeated in either realm! One cannot greatly minister in the spiritual things of God if his body is too incapacitated to allow him physical liberty. This is also acutely true if one is constantly harrassed and limited in the material sense.

1

Because the moving of the Spirit blesses us, we are prone to live by feeling rather than by faith. But without faith we cannot please God. My faith *must* be pleasing to God. Someone recently said, "God is not so concerned with the emotional, unstable Christians as He is with the *unbelief* in the stable Christians."[1] In this materialistic age we are surrounded by all the human heart craves. The believer no longer is required to exercise the faith that many believers in past years were, of necessity, required to exercise. Thus, faith, because it is not being exercised, is becoming powerless and impotent. Is this not the fear that the Lord expressed when He said, "Will the Son of man find faith when He cometh?"[2] He will find beautiful church sanctuaries filled with many people, but will he find faith? We have lending institutions to take care of financial emergencies. We have hospitals to take care of the sick. We have government agencies, ad infinitum, to take care of all of the other exigencies. Is it not still possible for all of these to be a great blessing to the church . . . but not at the expense of faith. Perhaps this will become our greatest challenge in the last days.

May this book inspire us to exercise our faith. Let us learn more perfectly how faith works. If faith is complex, then this presentation will not be helpful. We have endeavoured to reveal its utter simplicity. We have tried to stay with the application of the faith principles rather than to follow the hundreds of roads where the subject of faith would take us if one were to fully cover all that the subject involves.

The author would like to feel that this presentation will be a source of great strength and help to all that read it, but having had a few years experience, I will feel greatly rewarded by the Lord if these thoughts I share with you will be a blessing to even a few. Words cannot express the rich blessing and transforming effect that the confession of the Word by faith has been to me and my family. May we approach this great subject with open hearts, receptive minds and the effacing of all past failures "forgetting those things which are behind and reaching forth unto those things which are before."[3]

(1)   Dr. Howard P. Courtney
(2)   Luke 18:8
(3)   Philippians 3:13

# CHAPTER 1

# FAITH AND PRESUMPTION,

The heart's cry of the Psalmist was that the Lord would keep him from presumptuous sins.[1] Many have made an attempt to define what they thought the Psalmist meant. Certainly, whatever definition one accepts cannot take away from the fact that this was a sin that this great man desired to be free from entirely. Most all of us will recognize that to presume is to take for granted something you had no right to assume. I am sure we have all either experienced or have knowledge of someone who presumed, or assumed, that God was going to do something for him though he had no right to assume this. Why? Because he had not met the conditions of God's Word and therefore had no right to expect an answer. God has carefully laid out, in His Word, His conditions and what He expects from His people.

This leads us to a realm we must admit is unfathomably deep; that is the great subject as to what God can, or cannot do. Most all pentecostal believers know that God is a sovereign God and that man may have a choice to come in love and appreciation rather than coersion. He was given this choice by God, who in His love allowed man in the garden of Eden to exercise the free will with which he had been endowed. Thus in reality, God began to work with mankind with a restricted, planned form of sovereignty.

Not enough light has been shed on this major subject. Perhaps it is an awesome reverential fear that causes us to be fearful to the extent that we want to be the last ones on the face of the earth to have anything to do with debilitating the great glory of God Omnipotent. Many great sublime passages of scripture can be quoted to cause us to ever keep this uppermost in our minds. God is God, and we bow humbly before Him in awe and wonder.

This world has had such a shocking history of the dreadful sufferings of humanity that the theologians came up with the idea that perhaps "God is Dead" is a better explanation for the plight of the

(1)    Psalms 19:13

earth than to say He can't do a better job than the one being done. The final capstone of their plaint being the slaughter of millions of Jews in Europe. These are God's chosen people, therefore He must be dead!

The author recalls being with a young father as he stood over the casket of his infant two year old son. The father said, with a bitter overtone, "Why did God do this to us?" I was so glad I could tell him that he was blaming the wrong individual. I showed him the passage of scripture in Hebrews 2:14. It states that the devil is the one who has the power of death. When Job's children were destroyed, it was Satan who authored it.[2]

A friend of mine announced on a Sunday morning that his topic for the evening message would be, "Five Things That God Cannot Do." This immediately drew a lot of comment. There was quite a bit of commotion on the front row. Several people made such a scene that he inquired as to what was wrong. They replied that he could not preach on that subject because there wasn't anything that God could not do. He calmly reannounced his topic as being the same. They became so agitated that the pastor could see he would have to take some action. He said to them, "You really believe that there is nothing God cannot do?" When they positively reaffirmed this, he said, "Apparently there are some things that God cannot do, because He cannot make you pay your tithes."

Inasmuch as many theological books have been written as to the sovereignty of God, we will not add to it. Let us emphasize strongly that God has allowed man to play an important part in this life. God has given to mankind the complete responsibility for his soul and he will have to give account to God, on the judgment day, for decisions he has made and for the life that he has lived.

Perhaps the verse in John 1:12 will give us some insight on this great subject.

> "But as many as received Him, to them gave He power to become the sons of God."

Here is something that God has chosen not to do. He has chosen not to give salvation to anyone who does not receive Jesus Christ. In Revelation 3:20, Jesus Christ is pictured as being outside the door. If the door is opened He will come in. If it is not opened, He will not come in. If He did come in without the door voluntarily being

(2)    Job 1:7-12,19

4

opened, He would violate His own laws. This is one of the things that God will not do. He will not violate His own laws.

We can safely conclude that God is sovereign and, in His sovereignty, chose to restrict or limit Himself; that mankind might have a choice through Adam, the first man. Can any servant of God stand over a cancer-ridden , pain racked body and say to the suffering individual, "God could heal you if He wanted to, but He doesn't want to." This would say, in effect, that God did not have compassion or love. Is it not far better to tell them how much he loves them; how great is His compassion for them? He has given us His Word which shows us how to receive that which He provided for us through the atoning work on the cross of His Son Jesus.

"The atom bomb seems to have disturbed everything except the church. By overstating the sovereignty of God and blundering on in an atmosphere of stagnant dispensationalism, we safeguard our spiritual bankruptcy."[3] As this booklet goes to press, there are 35,000 pastorless churches[4] in the United States and may I vociferously defend my Heavenly Father and say it is not His fault. I believe that it is a sin of presumption to assume that we can sit back in indolent inactivity and by our action and by our words say that God is sovereign in the world; if the work does not go forward, it is His fault. The Bible says:

> "He is longsuffering to usward, not willing that any should perish, but that all should come to repentance.[5]

God's promises are always conditional. He can work where faith is exercised in His Word. Even Jesus, the Son of God, could not do mighty works in His own home town because of their unbelief.[6] *Is it not safe to believe that God is sovereign and yet believe that He can only work through the laws and methods that He has circumscribed in His word?* If we can strike this happy medium, perhaps it will better enable us in our endeavour to find the place of God's responsibility and the place of man's responsibility in the realm of the laws of faith.

What are His laws of faith? Are they complex and difficult? Are they simple enough that the wayfaring man, though a fool, need not err therein? If God's laws are so complex and difficult that only a

(3)    Ravenhill
(4)    Christianity Today
(5)    2 Peter 3:9
(6)    Mark 6:4-5

5

very few can comprehend them and only a limited few can receive, then the chances of winning men to Jesus Christ borders on the impossible. Thank God this is not so. God's love is so great and His Word so manifestly clear that the majority of converts and miracles happen on the mission field where the great truths of God are presented in the simplest form of discourse and ministry.

Great revivals were not preceded by profound theological discourse, but were the result of the simplicity of the presentation of Jesus Christ. May this book be so presented. May it not even begin to err in the taking away of any great truth of God and making it complex. Let us realize that an infallible, sovereign God has allowed fallible men the responsibility of the Great Commission. It has been said, "Because of this our praying needs to be pressed and pursued with an energy that never tires, a persistence which will not be denied and a course which never fails."(7) Finney once said, "Revival is no more miraculous than a crop of wheat." Jesus Christ is the only answer to a sick and dying world. As we do our part, God most assuredly will do His.

(7)    E.M. Bounds

6

# CHAPTER 2

# FAITH THAT PLEASES GOD

Without faith it is impossible to please Him.(1) What is this faith that pleases God? Notice that I didn't say, "the faith that pleases man". Which faith are you interested in? Some of the divine healing services that I have attended made me wonder whether the purpose of the evangelist was to magnify God or himself.

The faith that pleases God cannot always be seen by the congregation. It is not always made visible by a miracle that can be seen by human eyes. There are times when the Lord meets a person in the privacy of his own quarters, or some other place of prayer.

Because a person is prayed for in public and there is not a visible sign that he is healed does not unequivocally mean that God has not done something in his heart. That person might have had the faith that pleases God . . . and God met him but you and I might not have seen it.

I am vitally interested in the faith that pleases God.(2) In the Bible we have the definition of faith. One writer says: "Faith is giving substance to things hoped for."(3) This makes it easier for me to understand. The faith that I have is giving substance to the things that I need. We have asked the Lord to heal, or to do something for someone, and to do it immediately! Some people pray, "Lord give me patience, and I want it right now!" But faith is *giving* substance. It will come. It may not come instantaneously . . . but it will come, for faith gives substance to our hopes.(4) Sometimes our faith may have an insignificant beginning. God begins to do the work in our hearts. The substance is coming . . . but we give up too soon. We should not waver. Faith is giving substance to the things hoped for. We lose some of our most promising young graduates. They graduate from Bible College with honors. They go out into the ministry with high hopes and faith. Their faith is giving substance to their calling . . . but not fast enough! They are talented people . . . the progress is too

(1)    Hebrews 11:6
(2)    Hebrews 11:1
(3)    Newell
(4)    New English Bible

7

slow! They become discouraged. Oh, if only they would realize that their faith is giving substance to their "hoped for" ministry. Their ministry will develop! They must be made to understand that after they have done the will of God, i.e., answered the call of God, prepared themselves and gone out . . . then they need patience to reap and be blessed. *To say, "faith is giving substance" is to say that faith is progressive.* Faith that worked yesterday is not sufficient for today. The faith that works today will not be sufficient for tomorrow.

When an infant is born it has no knowledge of experience . . . only the potential to learn. Through life experiences it will grow and learn and someday be able to take its place in adult society. But it needs time to develop. The same is true, in a spiritual sense, of the growth of our faith. Many people will begin as a child of God . . . but they become discouraged with the rate of their growth. Let us endeavour to come to a greater understanding about faith so that we can see how it works. When you were saved, you exercised faith . . . but you did more than just believe. The man on the street believes. The drunkard, when asked about a belief in God, will answer in the affirmative. The Bible says that even the devils believe.(5)

All of these things serve to impress us that merely believing is not enough. There must be something else we did, then, to make our salvation experience effective. What was it? According to Romans 10:9, you not only "believed with your heart," but you "confessed with your mouth" that Jesus was Lord. Thus, you were saved. You exercised the kind of faith that pleases God. Your name was written down in heaven. *When you did thus, you linked together the two places that the Bible declares to be the location of our faith.*

> "The word is nigh thee, even in thy mouth and in thy heart: that is the word of faith, which we preach."(6)

So now we see that it was when you confessed what you believed you were saved. Now we are beginning to see how faith works. We believe something and we say so, or have corresponding actions. We will gladly tell the whole world that we believe. We have never seen God. We have never seen Heaven . . . but we confess that we believe these things to be reality. *The greatest miracle you will ever experience is the miracle of salvation. When you confessed what you believed in your heart, faith gave substance to reality, and you experienced the greatest of all miracles.*

(5)   James 2:19
(6)   Romans 10:8

8

Not only in Romans 10 does the Word have something to say concerning the mouth and the heart. In Matthew 15:8, Jesus made reference to the two together. Israel drew nigh to God with their mouth, but their hearts were far from Him. Hence their mouth and heart did not agree . . . making their faith barren and vain.

The Psalmist David said:

> "Let the words of my mouth and the meditation of my heart, be acceptable in thy sight . . . "(7)

Proverbs informs us that:

> "The heart of the wise teacheth his mouth and addeth learning to his lips."(8)

Ezekiel 33:31, Joshua 14:7, together with many other places in scripture, link together the heart and the mouth in the realm of active faith.

Another place in the scripture that has been a great source of help to me is James 1:26:

> "If any man among you seem to be religious and bridleth not his tongue, but deceiveth his own heart, this man's religion is vain."

We can paraphrase this same scripture, not changing its meaning, and it will read: "If any man among you is being religious in order to get something from God, and does not watch what he says, he will deceive (or contradict) his heart and he will not get anything from the Lord." Let us all learn a valuable lesson from the first lesson in miracles we experienced, the miracle of salvation.

Often I hear some good Christians say something very negative and I feel like interrupting to ask, "Do you believe that God can do anything you ask?" or, "Do you believe that God is able to meet your need?" I am sure he or she would reply, "Of course I believe." "Then," I would say, "why don't you confess that?" So many times we are unaware of the unbelief that we speak. When we do this, we contradict our heart and we waver from what we believe, and we cannot receive from the Lord . . . no matter how predisposed He is to help us. *He is restricted by our failure to 'confess with our mouth' what we "believe in our heart."* Thus our religious efforts are in vain. Let us go to the Old Testament for a good illustration of how this principle of faith operates. The first time that Israel came to the border of Canaan, twelve spies were sent to "spy out" the land.

(7)    Psalms 19:14
(8)    Proverbs 16:23

9

When they returned they came laden down with visible proof that all that God had said about Canaan being a land that abounded with milk and honey was correct. Of the twelve spies who went in, ten of them returned with a negative report of defeat and said they could not take the land. Two of the spies, Caleb and Joshua, believed that it could be done . . . and spoke their belief.[9] But the people believed the majority, and because of this display of unbelief, they had to wander forty years in the wilderness. Thus they were prohibited from entering the promised land until all who had not believed God were dead.

Now we see them once again coming to the border of Canaan. This time it is under the leadership of Joshua. Moses is dead. The Bible says, "he spoke unadvisedly with his lips."[10] The first great obstacle Joshua must face is the great, walled city of Jericho. How formidable it must have looked to the children of Israel! Awesome in height and wide enough, they tell us, that chariot races were held on top of it. They must have wondered if they heard Joshua right as he gave his commands. Could he have said they were to encompass the huge, walled city once a day for six days and then, on the seventh, not once, but seven times? It must have sounded like foolhardiness of the greatest degree! I am sure that if they had been allowed to express themselves they would have said, "This will never work!" "We'll never get in there!" "How foolish can we get . . . walking around out here in this hot sun!"

Joshua is going to teach them a great lesson in faith. A lesson that can profit us all. The lesson is this. *If you cannot speak words of faith . . . then do not say anything.* The Bible tells us that he had forbidden them to speak. They were not to utter a word.[11] They were to act their faith in silence. They really believed in their hearts that God would give them the victory. They believed that God would keep His word. Joshua knew that they believed in their hearts . . . and would not let them express with their mouths the negative doubts that they might feel for this moment.

For years I knew that it was "mind over matter" to say you were well when, in fact, you were ill. I knew it was, in actuality, not right to say you were not discouraged when you were! What to say! What to express in words was perplexing to me for years! It was not until I

( 9)    Numbers 13:30
(10)    Psalms 106:33
(11)    Joshua 6:10

heard a minister tell how he as a young boy was lying hopelessly ill and dying until the Lord taught him how to get his healing that I learned, the answer to the question of what to say when you are ill, discouraged, or afflicted. His testimony helped me. It corroborated what I had believed to be true for years. The answer is amazingly simple. Many people have stumbled over its very simplicity. The Lord taught this young man that the reason he was not getting his healing was that, when friends would ask him how he was, he would tell them that he was no better. It was not until he learned to *confess the word of God over his sickness* that his body began to mend. The answer, *believe the word* and, when people ask you how you are, tell them that "by His stripes you were healed." Tell them, "By faith I will be all right."

Some of you may ask, "Why emphasize what you *SAY more than what you believe in your heart?"* The answer is this! Most of us are taught to believe, from childhood, that there is a God. We already believe the Word. We already believe the gospel. What we have never learned, or been taught, is *to watch what we say*. Jesus said,

"For by thy words thou shalt be justified and by thy words thou shalt be condemned."(12)

Jesus again placed great importance on the words of our mouth when he said, "Ye shall have whatever ye say."(13)

This being true, it seems dangerous to me to hear so many Christians continually claiming God's inability to keep and protect them. They say such things as, "I guess I will die young, it seems to run in my family," or, "Father died of a heart attack, I guess I will too." Again, negating their ability in Christ, "I would like to teach a class, but I just can't do it." All negative statements and, inasmuch as Jesus said, "Ye shall have whatever ye say," statements that hinder us in receiving the benefits that are rightfully ours as children of God.

I have discovered that many ministers are very positive in the pulpit but very negative in the parsonage. They do not defeat themselves in the pulpit. They magnify the power and greatness of God. In the parsonage it is often another story. After expounding the power of God in the pulpit, they go home and tell the family that even God couldn't bring revival to this town! In some cases, pastors have ministered for years, moving from church to church . . . going

(12)    Matthew 12:37
(13)    Mark 11:23

through this cycle over and over again . . . never having realized that, according to Mark 11:23, they are only "having what they say."

When I hear believers say, "I am sick," or "I am not feeling well," I think of the scripture in Isaiah 33:24:

"The inhabitant shall not say I am sick."

We realize that this scripture context speaks of the millenium. May I remind us all that he who lives by faith in the Great Commission promises is already claiming the millenial promises by faith. Satan will be bound during the millenium and man will have complete dominion over him. He that by faith is living in the Great Commission promises has power to cast out devils. He has power over sickness. Many believers confess and talk about their sicknesses. Sometimes they do this to receive sympathy. Sympathy may be beneficial to one's emotional nature . . . but it will not bring healing. We who by faith live in the Great Commission millenial promises, shall not say we are sick . . . it is important to watch what we say!

What you say is important because the scripture says that the Lord Jesus is the High Priest of our confession.(14) Not the High Priest of our heart only. One has to believe before he is saved . . . so it is understood that he is now believing with his heart . . . so the word emphasizes the confession, with Jesus as the High Priest of our confession. This being the case, He cannot do much for a person having a poor confession.

I am sure the Lord Jesus is held responsible for many failures. Have you ever heard someone say, "I realy believed God for this answer to prayer, I wonder why He didn't do it?" or, "I asked God, but I guess He didn't hear me." That is their confession. That is what the Lord heard them say.

Our confession is also important relative to determining the will of God for our lives and the direction we should move. One may speak of acknowledging his ways to the Lord, then when he arrives at his destination and the prospects are not too hopeful, he may speak words of unbelief, words that express doubt as to whether or not he is where he should be. If we acknowledged our ways to Him and did not lean unto our own understanding in the move, then we must not undermine in our confession all that God is able to do for us. He is the High Priest of our confession. He heard us confess our doubts . . . and he cannot minister beyond what we say. The secret of determining the will of the Lord is to fully acknowledge our ways to the

(14)    Hebrews 3:1 RHM

12

Lord and then never waver. We can only confess that we have acknowledged our ways to Him and lean wholly upon Him and His Word, therefore we can know we are in His will. He looks ahead and sees all things . . . sees you standing secure in your faith and confession, and He works accordingly.

Dr. Duffield states in his book, "The Security of the Believer," "Man has a part to play in every spiritual transaction." This is most certainly true when we consider Him as the High Priest of our confession . . . and He ministers our confession before the throne. Perhaps this is why James tells us to be swift to hear and slow to speak.(15) We are infinitely more prone to speak quickly ... and so often no one seems to listen.

He is our High Priest of our confession in Hebrews 3:1. In Hebrews 4:14 we are admonished to "hold fast our confession."

Berkeley's translation states, "Let us cling to what we confess." The church of the Lord Jesus Christ must hold fast and cling to her confession of faith. Jesus said that on Peter's great confession of faith He would build His church. When Peter made his great confession of faith in Matthew 16:16, Jesus said, "Upon this rock," meaning upon this rock of his confession, He would build His church and the gates of hell would not prevail against it. Jesus Christ is building His church upon the confession of faith that He is the Son of the Living God. You and I, and all bloodwashed Christians that confess that Jesus is the Christ, the Son of the Living God, are making this great confession upon which He is building His church. When it is weak, irresolute, He cannot build His church. The true church, as contrasted against the false, can be judged by its confession.

The Bible teaches that we are to try the spirits whether they are of God. The true church confesses that Jesus is the Christ the Son of the Living God. Where this confession is lacking, we find the spirit of anti-Christ. One great organization that has come out strongly for the one world church has taken from their confession that Jesus is the Son of God.

Once, during one of our pastorates, I noticed in particular one lady as she came in to our church as a visitor. She entered into our worship service, sang the hymns and took part in the service as it progressed. After church, as she was leaving, I asked her about her church

(15)    James 1:19

13

affiliation. She informed me that she attended a spiritualist church. Being interested, I asked her to stop by the parsonage if possible, that we would like to converse with her further. That same week she came and during the course of our conversation, I found that she agreed with our doctrine. She believed in the sacrifice of Calvary. She believed in speaking with tongues. She believed in Divine Healing. As a young minister, I had to admit that I was baffled. Here was a very puzzling situation. I knew the Bible, and I knew spiritualist teaching well enough to know that our doctrines were not in harmony. Yet here was a believer in spiritualism agreeing right down the line with me! I was perplexed until suddenly the quickening of the Holy Spirit brought to mind 1 John 4:1-3. Remembering this, I asked her if she believed that Jesus Christ was the Son of God. Her immediate reaction was one of recoil. She said, "Oh no . . . we don't believe that."

This confession that Jesus is the Christ the Son of the Living God is not only the foundation of the church, but it is a confession of faith. Let our confession of faith be strong in Him . . . and let us hold fast our faith, let us cling to our faith without wavering.

What you confess is important because your heart, that with which you believe, can be strengthened by your confession. Haven't we often heard it said that, if you tell a lie often enough and long enough you will come to believe it? A story or incident recalled from the past and often recounted whether due to poor memory or growing exaggeration, very frequently becomes so distorted so as to no longer even be true! This fact has great significance when we relate it to speaking constantly the truth! Speaking the Word of God! Joshua 1:8 exhorts us to "Let not this law depart out of thy mouth." In other words, we are to constantly speak the Word.

Israel was not only commanded to love the Lord with all of their heart and soul, but they were to keep the Word in their hearts and to talk about it constantly. They were to talk of it sitting, standing, lying, walking - to talk of it to their children. Why? Because God knew if they talked of His Word, they would strengthen their hearts. Some people have talked negatively so long, they actually believe in their hearts that they are not able to do certain things.

Dr. Lillian Yeomans tells about a lady who came to her rest home. This lady was dying with tuberculosis, Dr. Yeomans put her to bed that first night and said, "Dearie, I want you to say, 'according to

Deuteronomy 28 that tuberculosis is a curse of the law . . . but, according to Galations 3:13, Christ has redeemed me from the curse of the law; therefore I can't have tuberculosis'." Dr. Yeomans taught this little frail, sick woman to repeat it until she had it fixed in her mind and memory. The next morning Dr. Yeomans asked her if she had said it and she said, "I must have repeated it a thousand times." She told the woman to keep saying it over and over. The glorious result was, that at the end of three days, the woman was restored to health. What took place? What happened here? She repeated it with her mouth, until she really believed it in her heart and when the two came together as one, she was completely healed and delivered.

Faith is the giving of substance to the things hoped for. Let us continue to speak our faith. Hold fast our faith and remember that He, the Lord Jesus Christ, is the High Priest of our confession.

There is an old saying, "Talk is cheap." Perhaps this is true . . . *But let us not cheapen talk. Make grounded, not groundless confessions. Your life grounded on the word . . . your conversation in the word.*

May I close this chapter by quoting from one of our finest pastors. "While I try my best to use my own talents, I know how very limited I am and how great the task, and power needed, to turn back the forces of Satan. When I confess the Word, doubt and unbelief flee. I do not only confess the Word to give me a positive attitude of mind, but to claim God's promises in my prayer life, thus assuring me the victories that Christ made possible."[16]

(16)    Reverend Eugene Kurtz

15

# CHAPTER 3

# FAITH THAT PROMOTES

Have you ever heard people say, "I guess I just don't have any faith," or, "Pray for me that I will have more faith." This is a common prayer request.

May we seriously ask the question, *"How does one get more faith?"* We have already established the great scriptural truth that "God has dealt to every man a measure of faith." We can safely conclude a man begins with faith as a gift of God. Some have termed it a sixth sense.

I am not in agreement with some that would encourage a person to go beyond their faith. Much serious damage has been done to our faith by the "so-called" faith healers. Their intentions might have been noble, but they have, in some instances, in their enthusiasm and the high emotional pitch of revival atmosphere, talked people into doing things beyond the limits of the individual's faith. They leaned toward the exploitation of faith, rather than the development of it. Let us, in this chapter, see how the faith that God has given to us *will promote more faith.*

Just a few months ago, the author experienced a great trial of his faith. Faith worth testing is faith worth having. The Bible speaks of the trial of one's faith as being precious. Shortly after this trial of faith, I was searching the scripture and looking up certain words in the Greek. I discovered a word in the Greek language, and I desire to share it with you here.

I am sure that most of us have heard of the Greek word "Logos." Most of us are familiar with this word as it is used in the writings of John,

"In the beginning was the Word," or "In the beginning was the Logos."[1]

The idea of a mind, a reason, a Logos ruling the world fascinated the Greeks; Plato declared it was God's Logos which kept the planets on course. The Stoics, who were at their strongest when the New Testa-

(1)     John 1:1

16

ment was written, loved this concept. It was Logos which put sense into the world. Philo, who was an Alexandrian Jew, promoted this word.(2) This word, Logos, as used by the beloved John, was a word charged with meaning and it made a great impact on the listener. W.E. Vine, in his expository dictionary of New Testament words, said that Logos is *the revealed will of God* and is used as the sum of the utterances of God. Strong's Concordance said of this word Logos that it is divine expression of God . . . page 45 of the Greek Dictionary of the New Testament. One could safely say, as he holds the Bible in his hand, that he is holding the sum total of the combined sayings of God . . . he has in his hand the *Logos of God.*

We must read the Bible to come to know the revealed will of God in our lives. To come to know personally the One in the beginning with God, who was the Logos of God . . . the Christ of God. As I became intrigued with the study of this word, I noted another term used in connection with it. Further pursuit revealed that not all Greek scholars agreed as to the full impact of this other word . . . "Rhema." Some scholars made the words "Logos" and "Rhema" very similar in meaning. But, in searching the works of many authors, I found that there is a striking difference. The fact that there are two words is significant . . .

We are first attracted to this word "Rhema" in Luke 1:37:

"For no word (Rhema) of God shall be void of power."

This indicates that "Rhema" as opposed to "Logos" is the singular saying of God, rather than the combined sayings of God. Jesus said in Matthew 4:4:

"Man shall not live by bread alone, but by every word (Rhema) that proceedeth out of the mouth of God."

In Ephesians 6:17, "Rhema" is used in connection with the sword of the Spirit. W.E. Vine states that this is not a reference to the whole Bible as such, but to the individual scripture. Adam Clark's Commentary, Volume VI, page 471, refers to it as "An ability to quote on proper occasions." Dr. Ironsides says of "Rhema" that it is not a picture of a man throwing the whole Bible at the devil . . . but of quoting explicit, fitting scriptures. This is also brought out in Dakes Annotated Reference Bible, page 212.

As I followed on in my study of this word, my excitement began to rise. I have known many people who have read their Bibles . . . they

(2)    Barclay New Testament Words

17

enjoyed reading their Bibles . . . but they seemed to lack faith. This provoked me to thought. Why is it that so many can read their Bibles and yet lack faith? Doesn't the Bible say that faith cometh by hearing and hearing by the Word?(3) What is wrong? It was with great excitement that I turned in my Bible references to find out whether the Greek word "Logos" was used in Romans 10:17:

"Faith cometh by hearing, and hearing by the Word of God."

. . . or if it would be faith cometh by "Rhema." If it is "Logos" then faith cometh by reading the Bible. This, of course, we must do. You must have guessed by now that I found the word to be "Rhema" . . . faith cometh by speaking the individual sayings of God. *Faith cometh by the quoting of the word of the living God.* "Rhema" is quoting "Logos." Faith cometh not by just reading the Word, which is "Logos," but by *speaking the word,* which is "Rhema."

Do Christians speak the word of God? May I use a humorous illustration? Let us go to a Wednesday night prayer meeting in a typical evangelical church. We've had a good lively song service, the leader then asks for a scripture shower. First of all, usually, there is a long silence. Then some dear, little saint of God remembers that she can quote the first verse of the 23rd Psalm. She does . . . and we admit that it is a wonderful verse of scripture. But what happens? Silently, to themselves about half of the congregation says, "There goes my verse." Next, some Sunday School child remembers that he has learned John 3:16. He quotes it, and the rest of the congregation says, "There goes my verse." Humorous? Yes, but it should not be so. To be so destitute of ability to speak the word, fitly, for every occasion or every trial of our faith, is to leave ourselves open to unlimited attacks of the enemy. The Christian is clothed with defensive armour. The only *offensive weapon* the Christian has is the sword of the Spirit, which is the Word of God (Rhema).(4) Faith cometh by hearing the Word. (Rhema)

When do we really hear the Word of God? This might be best illustrated by the example of what happens around the average household. The husband is about to leave the house, and, as he goes out the door, the wife calls out and asks him to come back by the store and pick up several articles. She mentions a list of three or four things . . . and he says he will bring them. But, having gone through this before, she wisely asks her husband to repeat the list back to

(3)    Romans 10:17
(4)    Ephesians 6:17

18

her average husband cannot do. He may remember the first one or two . . . but, more often than not, has forgotten the last. Do we really hear something if we cannot repeat it? Faith cometh by hearing . . . and, if you hear . . . *you can repeat it.*

This wonderful pentecostal faith that God has given us will promote more faith. Faith is not passive. Faith will go forward or backward. Jesus must have spoken with alarm when he asked if the Son of Man would find faith when he cometh.[5] Faith decreases in some, while in others it increases. When the disciples asked the Lord to increase their faith,[6] they echoed the cry of many human hearts. We need to increase our vocabulary in the Word of God. The believers faith, the answer to all generations, is going to become more vital as we approach the end time. In these last days of great temptation, we need power to overcome, even as Jesus overcame Satan in His hour of temptation. Jesus used the Word of God saying, "It is written . . . " Thus he overcame. We can overcome temptations, trials, discouragements. How? By hearing the Word (logos) and speaking the word (rhema).

(5)   Luke 18:8
(6)   Luke 17:5

# CHAPTER 4

# FAITH PROCEDURE

In Matthew 8:5-13, we have a tremendous example of great faith. This instance tells of a man, a centurion, who did not belong to the household of faith. He was a Gentile. At this time, prior to the death of the Lord Jesus Christ, there were very few Gentiles in the household of faith. But there were a few.

This man, no doubt, had heard about the Lord and might even have seen some of his miracles. He came to Jesus on behalf of one of his servants. Notice what the Word says:

> " 'Lord, my servant lieth at home sick of the palsy, grievously tormented.' And Jesus saith unto him, 'I will come and heal him.' The centurion answered and said, 'Lord, I am not worthy that thou shouldest come under my roof: but speak the word only, and my servant shall be healed. For I am a man under authority, having soldiers under me; and I say to this man, Go, and he goeth; and to another, Come, and he cometh; and to my servant, Do this, and he doeth it.' When Jesus heard it, He marvelled, and said to them that followed, 'Verily I say unto you, I have not found so great faith, no, not in Israel.' "

I am interested in this kind of faith because this is *the faith that caused the Lord to be well pleased.* This kind of faith arrested His attention. How wonderful it would be if the Lord God of Heaven would look down and the kind of faith in your heart would arrest His attention! Can you see Him turn to the angels of Heaven and say, "Behold the faith of that individual!" Because, the Bible says:

> "Without faith it is impossible to please God."(1)

The faith that pleases God is faith that this man had. In this illustration we have a faith that exceeds the average. This is not average faith we are talking about now . . . it is *above average faith.* We are not saying that everyone will have this kind of faith, but it is possible! Let us notice, in analyzing this man's faith, just what it was that caused the Lord Jesus to remark that he had not found this kind of faith anywhere else.

First of all, he understood authority. He talked in terms of authority. He was a man over men. He knew, to be successful, he had to exer-

(1)    Hebrews 11:6

cise authority. He knew the power of it. I am most certain that more people who are interested in faith would have a greater percentage of success if they understood the authority that is in the *Name of Jesus*. There is no one else in all the universe that we can approach who has authority comparable to the authority we find in the wonderful name of Jesus. The centurion had great faith because he understood authority.

Secondly, he recognized this *authority in Jesus*. This authority was not in His physical appearance; the authority was in His voice. When the soldiers returned who were sent to bring Jesus back from the Temple, the chief priests and Pharisees said, "why did you not bring him?" and they said "never a man spoke like this man."[2] The centurion recognized this authority in the Lord Jesus Christ. I don't know that he had heard about the Lord as He spoke to the turbulent sea, causing its violence to cease. I don't know how many miracles he saw; but he did recognize, in Jesus Christ, there was authority over the sickness that his servant had. I want you to notice, not only did this man know authority, and recognize it in Jesus, but when he came he came without *specification*. He was satisfied to leave the method and manner in His hands. Many times when we ask the Lord for something we have all pre-thought in our minds the manner in which we would like to see the answer to our prayer wrought. We would like to tell the Lord how to straighten out a lot of our problems. In other words, when we come to the Lord, we come with *specifications*. This man, this centurion whose faith so pleased the Lord that He marvelled, came to Jesus without specification.

Do you recall the time Peter was in jail and prayer was made for him by his friends? The saints had all gathered together and prayed earnestly for his deliverance. The Lord answered their prayer; sent an angel to release Peter from the jail. As Peter and the angel passed through the last gate, the Bible relates that the gate opened of its own accord.[3] Peter thought he was seeing a vision. I don't know whether he pinched himself, or if it was the cold night, suddenly, he came to the realization that he wasn't having a vision . . . he was free! He went immediately to the house where the people were praying, knocked on the door, and a servant girl answered. The girl was so overjoyed, that in her haste and excitement, she failed to unlock the door and let him in! She ran to the others and said, "Peter is here,

(2)     John 7:46
(3)     Acts 12:10

21

Peter is here. He's outside at the gate!" Their reaction was immediate. They said, in effect, "Hush girl, it can't be." At the servant girl's insistence, and Peter's continual knocking at the door, they finally went to see for themselves and, to their astonishment, there stood Peter!

I have heard some very fine ministers ridicule this and say, "These folk prayed, but didn't believe." They have tried to teach, from this instance, that if you pray long enough, whether or not you believe, God will hear your prayer. I don't believe this is what is taught here. The people who were praying for Peter did believe God. They would not have been praying if they didn't believe.

Therefore, you can rule out lack of faith right away. It was not lack of faith on their part. You say then, "Why didn't they believe the servant girl?" Because, when they prayed, they had *specifications.* They thought they knew how the Lord would free Peter. The next day they would have a court session and someone would stand up, as Gamaliel, and plead for Peter and the one under whose jurisdiction this case would come would release him. They had it all pre-thought, specifications all laid, as to how the Lord was going to answer their prayer to get Peter out of jail. But the Lord astonished them with His answer. He freed him in the middle of the night! They didn't believe that God could get Peter out of jail in the middle of the night. They weren't asking God to release Peter in that manner! When the answer came as it did, it astonished them. They prayed with faith, but the prayed with specifications in mind. When God answered their prayer, He did it in an exceeding, abundant manner, above all they could ask or think.[4]

The centurion who came to Jesus without any specification, came also to the Lord without *declaration.* He didn't declare His goodness. He didn't declare his righteousness. He didn't declare his liberality. He not only came without specification, he came without *declaration.* I have heard people say, good Christian people, "Oh, Brother Hicks, if anyone ought to get healed, Sister Brown ought to! She hasn't missed going to church in years and when she sold her house she gave half of the money to the Lord!" We run across this specification and declaration quite often. It becomes a stumbling block to faith when the answer doesn't come. It seems, sometimes, that if God answered prayer the way He wanted to, that people would not accept it. They would say, "Lord, I didn't think you were

(4)   Ephesians 3:20

22

going to do it that way. I don't know if I want you to do it that way or not." Our prayers are heard and answered . . . not on our goodness and not on our righteousness. They are heard and answered according to the righteousness of the Lord and our giving credence to His Word.

This centurion, a man of great faith, the faith that pleases God and caused the Lord to marvel, came in faith entirely based on *Jesus' word* saying, *"just speak the word."* That means he came without reservations or alterations. Without alteration whatever . . . no changes. We wouldn't rewrite the book if we could. Lord, you said it and we believe it is just as you said! I believe when we go to God in prayer and our prayer is based on His Word, it is prayer in faith that is powerful and pleasing. This is the kind of faith that causes Him to turn and say, "Look at that faith. They are believing Me just on the basis of My Word. They believe with simple, but powerful faith. No changes, no alterations. I will answer their prayer."

So many times people come to the Lord and, as the Lord listens to them, they have many alterations they would like to make. The faith that pleases the Lord not only comes based on His Word, without alterations, it comes also without *reservations.* This means that the centurion did not come to the Lord and say, "Lord, if this doesn't work, I'm going to try something else." This is what we mean by reservations. Many times people have in the back of their minds, "Lord, if You don't answer my prayer, I'm going to write a letter tomorrow and borrow one thousand dollars from a loved one." If the prayer is for healing, "If this doesn't work, I know a good doctor who has had success in this kind of a case." We are not belittling those who go to the doctor or those who borrow money. We are only specifying here that those who come to God on the basis of His Word will come without any reservation at all. They are not going to say, "Lord, if this doesn't work, I'll try something else." If an individual doesn't have the kind of faith so that he can come to God and trust wholly, without reservation, then he will have to use his reservations. Then, if he uses them, he must have had them in the first place.

We are not talking about what is wrong and what is right, we are talking about the kind of *faith that pleases God.* It comes to God, based on His Word and without alterations and reservations. I am not necesarily in favor of the action of one who, having had prayer for his eyes, goes immediately and destroys his glasses. I have seen examples of this and it is not necessarily a proof of faith. Not at all. Neither do I think that it is a lack of faith if he carries his glasses with him for a while or even wears them. We cannot judge that individual.

We are speaking of the reservations that some people may have. We are *emphasizing* the faith that needs no *reservations.* The faith that doesn't need a crutch to fall back on. The lady who believed that God was going to heal her of her lameness believed it to the extent that she sent her wheelchair home from the meeting before she was prayed for. She is an example of the kind of faith we are talking about.

This is the kind of faith that the centurion had. The kind of faith that caused the Lord to marvel and say, "Did you hear that? This man said it was not necessary for Me to even come . . . that I should just speak the word and his servant would be made whole! I haven't seen this kind of faith in all of Israel. It is well pleasing to Me!"

This kind of active faith that pleases God is also a witness to all. This kind of faith that can receive a miracle will testify to the world of the faith that comes to God without *alterations, declarations, and reservations.* This kind of faith was rewarded. So also will your faith be that pleases God. This is an excellent example of what our God given faith, the answer to all generaions, should be and can be. May it so become.

# CHAPTER 5

# FAITH THAT PROFITS

This great God given faith that is the answer to all generations profits the participants. It is of tremendous benefit to be a believer. The question is often asked, "Why are there not more Christians profiting by their faith?" Why is it that they seem to be buffeted by the same contrary winds that buffet the people in the world? There should be a benefiting and a profiting as a result of believing on the Lord Jesus Christ and being filled with the Spirit.

In many years of experience as a pastor, I have observed that many of the faithful members who attend church regularly are beset by trials and troubles. This should not be the portion of the child of God. We are not speaking here of the occasional trial and trouble that might come. We are speaking of the constant harrassment of the enemy that has them continually burdened with a sense of defeat. Dr. Narramore, in his book on The Psychology of Counselling, speaks of those who should not participate in church or Sunday School visitation because they have so many unresolved problems of their own.[1] We who enjoy the spirit filled life should be in a position to help others. *Our faith should profit us.*

Let us look in the scriptures to the book of Hebrews, chapter four, verse two.

> "But the word preached did not profit them, not being mixed with faith in them that heard it."

Is this possible? A group of spiritually-minded people, honest, sincere, listening to the Word of God regularly, yet not being profited by it. Yes, this is what the Word teaches. The church in the Old Testament, the children of God, heard the Word but did not profit by it. Not only did they fail to be profited by the Word that they heard, but actually were cut off and did not inherit the promised land.[2] We are also solemnly warned in verse one of this same chapter. Is it possible in this greater dispensation of Grace that we

(1)    Page 84
(2)    Hebrews 4:6

have people sitting and listening to the Word preached but not profiting thereby? I have known such people. They had heard literally hundreds of sermons and were not profited thereby. Their barren unfruitful lives bore witness against them.

Can we learn a lesson from this text? Yes, by doing what Israel failed to do. They did not mix the Word with faith inside them.

What is this failure? This failure of not being able to mix the Word with the faith that is in us? Adam Clark says that "this word mix is a peculiarly expressive word.(3) The ASV verse uses the word "blend." Williams translation states, "They were not, by faith, made one with those who heeded it." The ones who profited mixed the Word of the Lord with their faith. This we can do! We can hear the Word, read the Word; this is not sufficient. We must mix the Word! What is this mixer? Where does the mixing take place? Those spies who did believe saw the same enemies that the others saw. They saw the same huge walled cities. Yet they believed the Lord and *mixed their faith with the spoken word* and survived. *Their faith profited them.*

Let us use an Old Testament story of a woman who used her faith,and how she mixed her faith with what she believed. The story is found in 2 Kings 4. It is the story of Elisha and the Shunammite woman. He prophesied that this woman, who had befriended him, would have a son. This came to pass as was prophesied. After the child had grown up, it came to pass that he became ill and died. Did this woman of faith accept this apparent defeat? No. She did what we all should do when it seems that we are defeated. She refused to accept it! According to verse 23, when asked how things were, she answered, "It *shall be* well." She knew how to mix her faith and it profited her. Let us turn to the New Testament for another illustration in the Bible.(4)

Here we find the account of the woman with the issue of blood. This woman had not only suffered from the sickness, but also had suffered at the hands of the physicians and was growing steadily worse. She heard of Jesus and His power to heal and she believed what she heard, but she mixed her faith within her, for she said, "If I may touch but His clothes, I shall be whole."(5) This is the continuous tense in the Greek. Literally it means she said it and kept

(3)    Volume 6, Page 709
(4)    Mark 5:24-34
(5)    Mark 5:28

saying it. She put her faith into action and she was profited by her faith.

Can we be more specific? Can we spell out and locate this mixing process? Psalm 64:8, Septuagint version, states, "Their *tongue* has set him (God) at nought." Here we find a failure to mix, by correct speaking, the word with faith. Psalm 17:3:

"I am purposed that my mouth shall not transgress."

The prayer of the psalmist in Psalm 141:3 was:

"Set a watch, Oh, Lord, before my mouth, keep the door of my lips."

If we can accept it, *the speaking of words will often relate to the success or failure of the mixing process.* How often do you mix the word preached with the faith that God gave to you, the faith that is in your possession. An observation someone made about church members at Sunday dinner was, "Instead of the family having the preacher's sermon at dinner, they had the preacher." It may be that we heard the Word, but go our way and easily, even carelessly, forget what we have heard. If there is a mixing process that will cause the word and the faith to be mixed, the listener should learn what it is.

Israel was taught to speak the word.(6) They were to talk about it to their children when they were at home, when they were out for a walk, when they went to bed, and when they arose the next morning. This we should do also. One can, without any great difficulty, imagine what a powerful congregation would result if the subject matter of this chapter was practiced. Be diligent to mix the word preached, with faith. Speak often of the word preached. You will be profited.

(6)   Deuteronomy 6:7

# CHAPTER 6

# FAITH IS PRODUCTIVE

In the book of Philemon we have a verse of scripture that I think is one of the greatest verses in the Bible. This verse teaches a magnificent truth that seems to have gone unnoticed down through the years. I thank the Lord for this particular verse. It reads:

> "That the communication of thy faith may become effectual by the acknowledging of every good thing which is in you in Christ Jesus."(1)

I want you to notice that many people have overlooked or missed the value of this scripture, because it is in a context that has to do with philanthropic work, i.e., the charitable giving of this man. It seems that he was greatly used of the Lord to bless the saints, providing them with money and hospitality. You can take a verse out of context if it does not contradict with another part of the Bible. It must coincide with the rest of the scripture or it would not be proper to take it from context. This verse, however, is not really taken from context; it has a dual meaning. It is, of course, speaking about giving and makes a great missionary message. I want you to notice the wording of this "the communication of thy faith." Communication is usage. The exercising, or using, of your faith.

Communication is a word that is quite prevalent today. Therefore, we can paraphrase this by saying, "the using of your faith will become effectual." Notice that it says "thy faith. ' The scripture teaches that God hath dealt to every man a measure of faith.(2) God has given faith to all.(3) The Holy Spirit seems to place some emphasis on this. We should never under any circumstances confess that we do not have faith! When we do this, we deem God's Word untrue because He has given, or dealt, to every man a measure of faith.

Oh yes, faith can be covered and smothered. Unbelief can come in and it will so offset faith that a man may think that he doesn't have faith . . . but he does! It has just been covered, rendered useless. I

(1)     Philemon 6
(2)     Romans 12:3
(3)     Ephesians 2:8-9

think this is forcefully brought out at the deathbed of an atheist that held on to his atheism at the time of death recanted and confessed his error . . . others died screaming and cursing . . . knowing in their hearts they were soon to face God whose very existence in this life they had denied.

*Every human being has faith,* even the primitive native in New Guinea or Africa and the aborigine in Australia. They look into the heavens and there is a response in their hearts. Many times, according to their testimony after they have been saved, they have said, "I looked into the heavens and knew there was someone there." Of course, they cannot possibly know Who it is that causes this response because the Bible says:

> "How can they believe in Him of whom they have not heard and how shall they hear without a preacher and how shall they preach except they be sent."(4)

The Holy Spirit is literally saying, "The faith that you have, the faith that God gave you, can become effectual." This is a wonderful word in the Greek. This word means 'divinely energized.' The word itself suggests super-human energy,(5) effectual . . . or that which effectually worketh in you. *In other words, it is by divine energy that thy faith may become energized.* We are talking about the kind of faith that is able to restore that which has been destroyed. Actually, we are literally speaking of recreation here, because your faith can become so divinely energized that it can produce for you, or for whom you are praying, whatever is needed. This kind of faith can put the coin in the fish's mouth. This kind of faith can increase a little boy's lunch enough to feed a multitude.

Not too long ago we were talking with some of the ministers in our district. They related to us of how that 7 years ago they attended a large mass meeting. They were young and had taken their infant son with them to the meeting. Not realizing how long the meeting would last, they had taken only one bottle of feeding for the baby. The bottle was emptied long before the meeting was over . . . and when time came for the next feeding, the baby, as babies do, began to fret. The fretting soon turned to an angry, demanding howl and something had to be done. The man, one of our Four-square ministers, said, "I took the emptied bottle from my pocket, thinking that the baby could at least be pacified for a while. To the amazement of all

(4)   Romans 10:14,15
(5)   Word Studies - N.T. Vincent, Vol. 3, Page 517

around us, the bottle was full." This miraculous event happened not once, but twice, during the lengthy meeting!

The corroboration of this amazing tale was related to this same couple by a lady, as they were visiting in Alberta some time later. They were witnessing to this lady concerning the goodness of God and His care. She said, "You know, I was in Vancouver some years ago, and I attended some good gospel meetings . . ." and she went on to relate how she sat near a young couple with an infant and she witnessed how the baby's bottle was miraculously filled not once, but twice, enabling the young couple to remain in the service. They happily informed her that they were the people to whom she referred. This was confirmation!

This measure of faith can put milk in a baby's bottle. This faith can change diseased organs into healthy ones, can transform a small struggling church into a growing church. The word "effectual" means "that which worketh by divine energy." Many people's faith is not divinely energized; rather it is stagnant. It has not done much for them because *they have not exercised it . . . and they have not been positive.* They haven't been taught. They do not know the Word of God. They have not associated with people who have exercised faith in God and been positive. Contrariwise, they have heard much against people who have attempted to exercise faith. They will hear, occasionally, something along the line of, "Yes, I knew someone who refused to go to the doctor, who stopped taking his medicine . . . and he died."

Though there are many things we do not understand about the realm of faith . . . statements such as this will never be an aid to faith! It is very difficult to change habits of a lifetime, habits of wrong speaking that negate our faith in God's promises . . . especially if one has been told, by the doctor, that his case is hopeless and that he is going to die. Because of wrong teaching, many of God's people die prematurely. Too, there are some cases that we will never understand, in this life. *May God help us to leave alone the things we do not understand and receive benefit from the things we do understand!*

Notice that it says, "Your faith will become effectual." How? By the acknowledging! This acknowledging will result in evident action. This implies confession as well.

Dr. Nathaniel Van Cleave and I perused his library of Greek word studies. The word "confession" comes as close to the meaning of "acknowledging" as any that could be found. If you say something to me and I acknowledge it, I usually do so by speaking to you. If you call me on the phone, I acknowledge by answering. If I am not home, I acknowledge by returning the call. So then, we see that the word implies speaking. Speaking what? What are we going to acknowledge, speak, confess? Is it going to be our weaknesses . . . and God knows we all have them! Is it going to be our inabilities . . . we all have them! Is it going to be our disappointments? Who among us has not been disappointed! People, suffering disappointments, are prone to speak or acknowledge negative things. Oh, yes. They are there. We do not deny this. There are many things of this nature . . . but why talk about them! I would rather talk about my victories in Christ. Talking about defeat will not help me . . . and they certainly won't help you!

The majority of people, the majority of the time, seem to talk of things they cannot do or yesterday's failures! On the subject of sickness . . . they talk themselves into the hospital! On the subject of finances . . . they talk themselves into bankruptcy! On the disappointments of life . . . they talk themselves into despondency! *What should they say!* Why not thank God for the good things they enjoy, for their health, for the happy circumstances of life that is theirs! Why constantly acknowledge weaknesses, sickness, and despair? When you ask someone to take a Sunday School class, more say "I can't" than say "I will." You may be able to talk him into it, but he will likely continue with the theme "I can't."

Sometimes people are motivated to say this to receive sympathy or attention. An individual will sing a vocal solo in a church service. At the close of the service, as you compliment him on his selection, you will hear him answer, "Oh, I just did terrible! I shouldn't even have been up there!" He doubtless does not really believe that . . . but if you agreed with him you would probably lose a friend!

Let us bring this into the realm of faith. It takes on a deeper meaning. God is not asking us to acknowledge our weaknesses. He is not asking us to say an untruth or as some may teach, "mind over matter," but He is asking us to *"acknowledge every good thing."* I praise the Lord that, years ago and by His divine help, I decamped the negative realm for the positive realm. I don't want anything to do with living in the negatives of life. Satan can sow the seeds of trouble, but it is up to us to see that he has a crop failure! Someone has said that you can't keep trouble from coming in the door . . . but you

31

don't have to offer it a chair. The negatives will come. We will have them with us. But, thank God, we can deal with them. In Christ Jesus we are more than conquerors.

Notice that our faith will become divinely energized by the acknowledging, by talking about, by the confessing, of every good thing which is in you in *Christ Jesus*. What am I to talk about? What am I to acknowledge that will cause my faith to become effectual? I am going to talk about what is in me because of Christ Jesus. I am sure that the wonderful verse of scripture is familiar to you which says:

> "Ye are of God little children, and have overcome them: because greater is he that is in you that he that is in the world."(6)

You see, I have Jesus Christ in me. It is by faith, but faith is the most powerful force in the world. By it the worlds were framed. They remain ever there and swing in their constant orbit since God spoke them into being.

We are talking about the kind of faith by which Christ indwells our hearts. You can't see it . . . but it is there. You can't see the billions of molecules, neutrons, and protons that are revolving around in a piece of wood, but they are there. Therefore, it ought to encourage our hearts that *this faith that God gave us can become effectual, or divinely energized in us, by the acknowledging of what God has done for us.* This is why it is wrong for the believer to say "I'm sick" or "I am defeated," or "I am discouraged." The Bible tells me I am healed, and that "I can do all things through Christ."(7) *It is up to me which one I will acknowledge.*

It is wrong for me to say I am well if I am suffering. That would be an untruth. If you ask me how I feel, and I may be suffering various symptoms, I will not tell you I feel all right. I will tell you,

> "By His stripes, I am healed,"(8)

or "By faith I will be all right." When I do this, I acknowledge the positive . . . and not the negative. When I acknowledge the positive, I acknowledge every good thing which is in me which God has given me because of Christ and my faith becomes divinely energized. As one doctor put it, the cells of our body respond to our speaking.(9)

It is no wonder Jesus said to the woman:

(6)    1 John 4:4
(7)    Philippians 4:13
(8)    1 Peter 2:24
(9)    Dr. Rebecca Beard

32

"Go thy way, thy faith hath made thee whole."(10)

That is why it is important that we acknowledge the faith that is in our hearts. That is why it is important that we acknowledge every good thing which is in us in Christ Jesus. Dearly beloved, this is a gem in the overall riches of the Bible.

If we are born of a family where we inherited inabilities, timidity, fear, or many other inhibitions that could be named, we can take heart . . . God is able to change this. People who have inherited timidity and introversion are transformed by the miracle of conversion. After they are saved and become filled with the Holy Spirit, and they begin to exercise this God given faith, they can preach and minister with authority. The Christ is in them. They can say with Paul:

> "I can do all things through Christ which (who) strengtheneth new."(11)

You can become effectual, you can do a work for God. God can literally change you.

> "If any man be in Christ, he is a new creature . . . old things are passed away, behold all things are become new."(12)

This verse can help a multitude of people in our churches and in the ministry who are prone to acknowledge their weaknesses and inabilities. If they would change and begin to acknowledge every good thing which is in them because of Christ Jesus, they would not fall behind in anything because God has given great gifts to the church. He will give you the gifts that you need. Your faith can become divinely energized by the acknowledging of that good thing which is in you in Christ Jesus. Do you want your faith energized? Do you want to see God do things through you? *Watch what you acknowledge,* lest your faith lie dormant within you . . . lest your faith does not become "energized."

> "That the communication (usage) of your faith may become effectual (may work by divine energy) by the acknowledging (confession) of every good thing (not negative thing) which is in you in Christ Jesus."(13)

Go your way, only speaking that good thing which is in you in Christ Jesus, which you must surely believe in your heart, and need to say with your mouth.

In conclusion of this chapter, may I quote from one of our finest missionaries: "To speak what the *Word* says about us, or a particular

(10)    Mark 5:34
(11)    Philppians 4:13
(12)    2 Corinthians 5:17
(13)    Philemon 6

situation, makes all the difference in the world. When we speak, we speak our own feelings and as our mental logic would dictate. To talk about my weakness or sickness does not build up my fellowman and usually is to gain *self attention.* I am convinced that it is the saying or *Speaking of the word that is the real victory.* I was thrilled to hear you remark while at camp that you were not advocating plain, positive speaking . . . but rather, a confession of our position in Christ and our relationship to Him. I can say that I have been free from sickness and my family blessed through our refusal to claim and diagnose our symptoms . . . but rather speaking what God says in His Word about these things. I can only wish that I had been guided along these lines when I first started out in the ministry."(14)

(14)     Reverend Mason Hughes (Missionary to New Guinea)

34

# CHAPTER 7

# FAITH THAT PREVAILS

I do not desire to be numbered among those ministers who leave the impression that if a person has faith, all will be supernal and the future always bright. Much damage has been done to our Christian faith by these "hobby-horse riders." They attempt to inspire climactic faith in one series of meetings that will draw large crowds and bring in ample finances.

I have been in these services and heard ministers make great declarations that not only excite the imagination, but leave the impression that if your faith doesn't rise to the occasion that the individual is lacking. I have seen the sick and infirm join the healing line, move across the platform, and if they are not healed visibly, suffer public abuse at the hand of the evangelist. Let us be truthful. Sometimes our faith meets seemingly immovable barriers and then we need the kind of "faith that prevails" against all of the mountains that stand in the way of spiritual and physical progress. The Lord knew that we would need an example of the kind of faith that prevails, and included this illustration which we will now consider. It is the account of the Syrophoenician woman who came to the Lord, seeking help for her daughter.[1]

Racial prejudices have always existed in the world. There has never been a time in history when they did not exist. This Syrophoenician woman knew in the natural, and so did the disciples that she had no socially acceptable reason for coming to the Lord. If you read it carefully, you will see that she had a difficult time getting through the disciples to get to the Lord. Finally, the disciples became wearied with the woman continually annoying them and they said in effect, "Lord, we want you to take care of her; we can't do a thing with her. We have tried to send her away, and she is back here again." She fell down at Jesus' feet and said, "Oh, Lord, have mercy on us." Her daughter, you will recall, was vexed with a devil. The Lord said to her, "It is not right to take the bread from the children and give it unto dogs."

(1)    Mark 7:25-30

35

Why did the Lord speak thus to her? He spoke thus because it was the kind of language she understood. In other words, He was saying to her, "Woman, don't you realize that you are not entitled to this? Don't you know that you are a Gentile and we are Jews? Don't you realize that what you are asking for is difficult? Do you not realize, woman, how much boldness you exercised by coming here, asking me to take the bread from the children's table and give it to dogs?" But this woman had the kind of prevailing faith that demanded an answer to her plea. This woman had the kind of prevailing faith that you and I need the kind of faith that will not become discouraged and quit. This woman looked up to the Lord and said, "Yea, Lord, but the dogs get the crumbs that fall from the table." The Lord answered, "Great is thy faith." I don't know all that He said the Bible doesn't record all of His words, but He must have turned to His disciples and said, "Did you hear that? This woman has great faith." *The kind of faith that did not interpret delay as refusal; the kind of faith that was not easily offended.*

This woman did not have self pity. She had compassion for her daughter. She was there, not to get something for herself, but on behalf of someone she loved. You see how her faith secured healing and deliverance for her daughter. Prevailing faith is born of great compassion and love. It is in the absence of compassion and love that faith is easily rebuffed. It is in the absence of compassion and love that faith easily tires. I read of a mother whose daughter was blind. For fourteen years the mother kept praying and saying, "I know that some day you will see." The miracle came to pass, even though it took fourteen long years.

*Prevailing faith is born of great humility.* This woman's faith was not rebuffed by reference to her social standing or her race. She humbled herself at the feet of One who, in the natural, she would despise. As I delve more deeply into God's word, I realize how much pride interferes with our receiving anything from the hand of God. There is not much doubt that what the Lord Jesus said to this lady was said in order to test her. She passed the test. The Bible teaches that we are to humble ourselves.[2] This we must be able to do or the Lord would not have asked us to do it. It also says he gives grace to the humble.[3] You are more apt to be truly humble when others think you are and you think you are not.

(2)    2 Chronicles 7:14
(3)    James 4:6

36

Notice that "prevailing faith" will *project itself into action*. She had to go to great lengths to receive. I have had people say that the reason they did not come up for prayer at the close of the service was that there was no mention of their particular affliction. Had it been mentioned they would have responded. Prevailing faith is faith in action. This is vividly illustrated by the four men who brought their friend to Jesus. When the press of the crowd kept them out of the house where Jesus was preaching, they proceeded to the roof whereupon they tore a hole large enough to let the sick man down into the presence of Jesus. The word teaches that when Jesus looked up *He saw their faith*. We can say that *prevailing faith is visible faith*.

Prevailing faith is unwavering faith. She did not give up when she was not able to get past the disciples to the presence of Jesus. I recall, very vividly, a time when I was tempted to waver. We, as pastor and church, had made an "all out" effort to be faithful in putting our missionary giving first. The church had accepted the challenge of not only giving personally through the faith promise method, but also had agreed to give all of the offering that came in on Missionary Sunday to Missions. Needless to say, when a church and pastor agree to do this, they will be tested. On a Saturday night we, as a church council, were told by the secretary-treasurer that we were in the red. The next day was Missionary Sunday and, of course, it was obvious that we urgently needed to have an offering for our church expenses. To say that I was tempted to waver is an understatement. I remember being ready to walk on the platform to begin the morning service, still debating in my heart what I was going to do. I had no more than made up my mind not to waver and to go ahead and give all the offering to missions as usual, when one of the members opened the door of the anteroom and handed me an envelope. In the envelope were two checks. One for a thousand dollars for the church and the other a check for seven hundred fifty dollars for missions! I would like to say I have always exemplified this kind of faith, but I cannot. When I have, the Lord has always been faithful to honor His Word. *The faith that is unwavering prevails.*

37

# CHAPTER 8

# FAITH AND PRAISE

At a recent convention one of the speakers electrified the audience with this apt description, *"Praise is faith in action."*(1) This statement is a great truth. a truth that begins in the Old Testament and is carried on over into the New Testament. The early New Testament believers were described as "Praising God, and having favour with all the people. And the Lord added to the church daily such as should be saved."(2) God's people, who have His Spirit, enjoy praising Him. Praise will keep them in touch with God. Can we safely assume that the more intimate the fellowship between man and God, the more he will praise Him? You will always notice that when a Charismatic church begins to diminish in their praise to God, the more they will turn to programming and the spectacular.

God inhabits the praises of His people.(3) He must, therefore, enjoy hearing His people praise Him. The first encounter one has with a Charismatic church that praises God can be an unusual experience, especially if he formerly attended a church which had a liturgical form of worship. Many have remarked, after having become familiar with this kind of worship service, that it was very difficult for them to learn to raise their hands and praise the Lord aloud for the first time. This should not be a surprise to us. *That which produces power and draws one close to God will be opposed by both the enemy and the flesh.* The enemy of our soul seeks praise and worship for himself, therefore, it is only natural for him to oppose praise that belongs to our Heavenly Father. The flesh will oppose this spiritual ceremony by putting up a formidable barrier to every spiritual step and exercise. Praise is faith in action because we are praising one whom we have never seen. Therefore *praise and faith* are intricately tied together.

The Lord Jesus Christ, in one great statement, placed His stamp of approval on *praise.* His followers were praising Him with a loud voice. The bystanders were very critical, most of them being of the established religious order. They said to Jesus, "Master, rebuke thy

(1)    Dr. Joseph Knapp
(2)    Acts 2:47
(3)    Psalms 22:3

disciples." Jesus answered and said unto them, "I tell you that if these should hold their peace, the stones would immediately cry out."(4) What a tremendous first lesson we learn here by observing the *uniting of praise and faith*. Notice that the *disciples praise the Lord in the face of unbelief*. Unbelief was all around. Their ears were assailed by many adverse statements concerning the Lord. One who praises the name of the Lord, when unbelief is on every hand, demonstrates *faith in action*. The author experienced one of the greatest miracles in his life by lifting his voice in praise in such a circumstance.

Secondly, *They praised the Lord in the midst of confusion*. One has only to read the above passage of scripture and use his imagination a little bit to see clearly that this situation, a babble of contradictory cries, was seething with confusion. A good time to praise the Lord! How contemporary this thought is in these present days. When confusion presses in on every side and closes in with a deafening roar, let us lift our voices in praise to God. He is not confused, and is able to lead us out of confusion.

Thirdly, *The disciples, on this occasion, were praising the Lord by faith*. He was not yet crowned King. He was not yet on the throne of David. The Roman rule was not yet overthrown. Yet they believed in and praised the Lord by faith. Not only are we to praise the Lord by faith but, if faith is not present . . . praise the Lord anyway and you will soon have a witness of your faith! Your faith will leap into action! When the heavens seem as brass, praise the Lord! When there seems to be no way out, praise the Lord! Learn this great truth and practice it . . . to your good and God's glory.

Now let us notice what the Lord said their praise by faith accomplished. *Their praise, in the face of unbelief and confusion and being offered in faith, was more powerful than the elements*. Jesus said (paraphrasing) that if they were silenced the elements would protest. Elements do seem to combat us. They rise up in the form of those things that cause sickness, discouragement and formidable barriers. But, thank God, *praise* dominates the barriers of elements. The next time you feel the elements are trying to close in on your spiritual life, *praise the Lord*. One medical doctor gave an entire chapter of her book to the subject, "The Praise Cure."(5)

Are we afraid of what people will think when they enter our doors?

(4)    Luke 19:37-40
(5)    Dr. Lillian Yeomans "Healing from Heaven"

39

Are we afraid we will lose some of our more liberal givers if we begin to encourage praise to our Heavenly Father? If we have an atmosphere of praise when people first enter our church, then we will not have to face a fear of losing them later because they were not exposed originally to this integral part of worship. Lifting our hands in the sanctuary and praising the Lord is as scriptural as finding salvation. Let us "lift up our heart with our hands unto God in the heavens."(6) "Lift up your hands in the sanctuary, and bless the Lord."(7) May we close with this great verse:

> "Who so offereth praise glorifieth me; and to him that ordereth his conversation aright , will I show the salvation of God."(8)

Not only do we see here that faith and praise are united, but the cultivation of our "right speaking" is encouraged. The ultimate in "right speaking" is our conversation that praises and glorifies God. Certainly *praise* is the highest declaration of faith! Praise is faith in action!

(6)    Lamentations 3:41
(7)    Psalms 134:2
(8)    Psalms 50:23

40

# CHAPTER 9

# FAITH THAT PREEMPTS

Is it possible that unbelief is a robber? A robber of the power of the Holy Spirit that is needed to meet the needs of this generation. Can unbelief be found among God's people? Can it reside side by side with faith in the believer's heart and rob him?

In the Bible we have the illustration of a great need in a family. A member of that family was vexed by the enemy. Surely this was a great need. This distraught father heard about the healing ministry of the Saviour. He brought his little boy to the Lord Jesus and asked Him to heal him. When Jesus asked him if he believed, the man said, with tears in his eyes, "Lord I believe, help thou mine unbelief."[1] By this we can see that it is possible that *faith and unbelief can reside in the same heart.*

May we safely assume that Israel believed in their God? Their God had wrought so many miracles for them! Was He not a God of miracles? Did they not believe in Him? Surely we can be safe in assuming this! Yet in Scripture we find that they could not enter into the promises of God because of unbelief.[2] Perhaps the language of the word might have been softer if the Lord had said, "They did not believe." Unbelief is a harsh word. For one to confess that they do have unbelief is a difficult thing. We do not hear many such admissions, yet this is the language of God.

The possibility of unbelief becoming part of the spirit-filled believer's heart staggers us. The possibility of it going undetected staggers us even more! Yet it became a reality in Israel. It took over and robbed them of their faith in God. They failed to enter in because of this fact. If unbelief can become a dominant power in the heart of a believer,[3] if it can slowly take over until it drives out faith, then we must recognize the urgency of having to deal with it. It is deadly. It can rob us. It can rob God in that He cannot pour out on His people the blessing that He desires. It is only as we see un-

(1)    Mark 9:23,24
(2)    Hebrews 3:19
(3)    Hebrews 4:6

belief as the robber that it is, that we will be able to learn to deal with it, to rid ourselves of it, before we follow the same path that led the people of Israel away from God.

Before we go on to some examples of unbelief in the Bible and the prescription for unbelief, let us make one more indictment against unbelief. *Notice that the Bible calls it evil.* Evil is the opposite of all that is godly. It is diametrically opposed to righteousness.[4] It does not come from God. It has, therefore, no part in Him. Evil comes from Satan, from this present evil world, from materialism, from other sources . . . but not from God.

Unbelief causes men to say the ways of God are not necessary. There are people in the world, not living for God, who believe there is a God. You can ask them, "You say there is a God, then why do you gamble, drink . . . why are you living for the world rather than for God?" They often will say, "Well, I just don't believe those things are necessary ... going to church, tithing, teaching in Sunday School, etc."

Therefore, he reveals that unbelief is in his heart. Unbelief concerning the scriptures that tell us we are to go to church, to give to God and other services we render to Him.

Remember the time that Naaman the leper heard about the prophet in Israel? Naaman was the captain of the Syrian army. He travelled a long journey to come to this prophet. He had heard, through a captive Israelite maid, that this prophet had great power with God. He felt that if he could get to the place where this great prophet could pray for him, he would be healed. Because of the enmity that prevailed between the Syrians and the Israelites, Naaman presented himself to the king in peace . . . either a white flag, a banner, or a courier who went before him proclaiming that this was a mission of peace.

At the king's inquiry as to his presence, Naaman answered, "I am here to be recovered of my leprosy." Those who were listening agreed that it was Elisha that he sought . . . and, eventually, Naaman found himself at the house of this man of God.[5] There he stood outside his door. Word was sent to Elisha concerning the reason for Naaman's long journey. Word was sent back to Naaman instructing him merely to go dip into the River Jordan seven times. Naaman,

(4)    Hebrews 3:12
(5)    2 Kings 5:9

42

this mighty captain of the Syrian army, would never have made that long journey across the desert and mountains if he had not believed what that little girl said about the prophet and the God of Israel!

You cannot say he had a heart of unbelief. He did believe or he would not have made that long and arduous journey. He did believe what he was told about the prophet. You can almost see Naaman as his anger rises and he becomes wroth at the suggestion that he should dip in the River Jordan when he had rivers in his own country! Why, he had already dipped in various rivers many times . . . but had not been recovered of his leprosy! Finally, after a time, someone was able to calm him and reason with him. He was made to see that Elisha had not asked him to do a difficult thing . . . perhaps if he had, Naaman would not have hesitated to do it. Naaman finally agreed to do as the prophet had instructed. Unbelief was allowed to rise in his heart but, by obeying God's will through the voice of the prophet, *he overcame that unbelief by obeying the word!* Isn't that good? Well, you know, the rest of the story. He went, dipped as he was told, and when he rose up out of the water the seventh time . . . his flesh was clean, uncontaminated any longer by leprosy. Unbelief will sometimes rise up in our hearts and cause us to say that the ways of God are not necessary. It will rob us of blessings as it almost did Naaman. Naaman overcame unbelief by obedience to the Word of God through the Prophet.

Then, again, unbelief will cause men even to laugh at the ways of God. You remember, on the day of Pentecost, when the disciples were filled with the Holy Ghost, and those who were on the outside who heard the noise and commotion, came near and laughingly said, "These men are drunken."(6) Remember the time that Sarah laughed. Sarah, an old woman of almost one hundred years of age, and God said she would have a child! She laughed.(7) God said, "Did I hear Sarah laugh?" She answered, "No, I'm not laughing." But she was. It was funny to her. I don't know if it was momentary unbelief or not, in her heart, that caused her to laugh. At any rate, through faith in their hearts, eventually they did have a child. I am only pointing out that unbelief will not only cause us, as it did Naaman, to say the ways of God are not necessary. It will also cause us to say the ways of God are foolish, and perhaps even laugh at the ways of God. *Unbelief will cause the destruction of the soul and body.* We think of

(6)    Acts 2:13 (NOR)
(7)    Genesis 18:12

43

Lot and his sons-in-law when the word came from the angel that they were to flee from Sodom and Gomorrah. Lot believed. His two daughters with him believed and did not look back. But his wife did look back. Apparently she did not believe that she would turn to a pillar of salt. But this same unbelief caused her destruction. Unbelief also caused Lot's sons-in-law to refuse to leave Sodom and, because of it, they were destroyed. Unbelief is a terrible robber. It robs us of the things of God.

Let us explore this further. Not only does it rob us, it robs God. You see, God is our heavenly father. Much of the joy and happiness and pleasure that is God's, is His as a *Father*. He is pictured in the Bible as a Father.(8) He is pictured as a Father who enjoys His family . . . His children. The joy of God is in His children, much the same as any parent. When God's children are happy, when His children are enjoying His blessings, God is happy. When an earthly father sees his children unhappy, it makes him unhappy. The same is true of our heavenly Father. Our Father God in Heaven looks down upon us many times and, because of the unbelief that robs us of pleasure, He is robbed of the pleasure of seeing His people happy. Use your imagination with me now. How do you think I would feel if I over-heard my daughter say to a neighbour child, "You know, I just don't know what we are going to do at my house. I don't know if I will have a place to sleep tonight or not. I don't know if there will be any food for breakfast. I'm so worried I can't sleep." How do you think that would make me feel? It would certainly make me to appear to be a very poor father, and not a good provider for my family. If I saw my daughter was worried or concerned in any way that I could not take care of her needs, it would rob me of happiness. Just so, it robs God. God looks down upon His family and sees worry, fear, and ungrounded concern many times. He can hear Christians as they say, "I just don't know what I am going to do." Have you tried praying about your problem? "Oh, I wouldn't want to bother God . . . I wouldn't want to bother him with my problem."

All the while here is our Heavenly Father, with a heart of love and power unlimited, ready to reach down and help His children so they might be happy . . . that they might be joyful. Unbelief robs them; it also robs God. Oh, it must be so pleasurable to God when one of His children asks Him for something, believes Him for it, receives it, and goes testifying of it! God rejoices in this!

(8)    2 Corinthians 6:18

44

Volumes could be written of God's people who have suffered needlessly. Israel alone is example enough. Have you ever stopped to think how it must have affected God when He led the children of Israel through the wilderness after delivering them from the Egyptian bondage by His great outstretched arm. Here He leads them, by Moses, over to the Promised Land. Because the spies, ten of them, brought back an evil report of unbelief, God had to turn away that great nation. Literally they turned themselves away, by their unbelief. They wandered in the wilderness for forty long years, until every individual above the age of twenty died. God was robbed of the joy in seeing His children in Canaan . . . and His children were robbed in not being able to go in and take the land.

We think of God's people today. We think of many who live in poverty and suffering in many areas of the world. God is not happy about this. *The Bible says that Jesus came that we might have life and have it more abundantly.*(9) It isn't abundant life to have to wonder where your next meal is coming from. It isn't abundant life when you are worried over bills you are not able to meet. Of course, I could say here, in quotes, that neither is it God's will that we go out and get ourselves in more debt than we can manage! I may not hear many "amens" on that, but the Bible says, "Owe no man anything."(10) What we are really talking about here is God's people living in peace and tranquillity, walking in obedience and, because of this, their faith appropriating the things of God. But unbelief comes along and it robs God. It robs God's people of the necessities of life.

It is even possible that unbelief could get in and ultimately rob a person of his standing with God. No, we are not of the group that believes "once in grace, always in grace." We don't believe that once you get in, it is impossible to get out. We don't believe this because, if this were true, a man could be saved by one moment's believing, and whether he believed it or not for the rest of his life would be irrelevant . . . he would still be saved, would still get to heaven. This is not acceptable to most of God's people who are Bible students; who recognize the admonitions to be holy, and to walk prayerfully with God. These things would not be necessary if a person, by one moment's believing entered the family of God and kept that status the rest of his life, regardless of what he did thenceforth. No, we do not believe this is the way. We do believe that a person can depart from

( 9)    John 10:10
(10)    Romans 13:8

45

the faith.[11] The Bible teaches this. I am not going into a lengthy discourse on "once in grace, always in grace," except merely to point out that we do believe that people can fall away. In fact, in Hebrews it says it is impossible to renew them again to repentance. They fall away seeing they crucify to themselves the Son of God and put Him to open shame.[12]

It is possible then, that a person could get away from God, not turn back to Him, and be robbed of a home in heaven. Unbelief in an individual can cause him to become disinterested in the gospel work. I call it "gospel fatigue." One can just grow weary of well doing, tired of going to church . . . just tired! It has to be unbelief. Unbelief that enters into the heart of an individual and causes him to say that the ways of God are not necessary.

Unbelief will also rob a person of his joy. The Bible says that the joy of the Lord is our strength.[13] Much of our Christian strength comes from the joy of the Lord. This is why I like to hear people sing. Did you know that you can sing yourself into a state of happiness? Try it sometimes. You get up in the morning, look at yourself in the mirror and it scares you. You feel as badly as you look. Start singing! I am not just saying this. Try it! It will make you feel better. Oh, you say, "I don't feel like singing." Sing anyway. If you don't feel like singing, sing all the more fervently! The first thing you know, you will begin to feel better. It is a wonderful thing to sing and to praise the Lord. We will deal more with this subject when we discuss the cure for unbelief.

Frustrations, nervous tensions, so many things that cause troubles in our digestive systems, are all the products of unbelief. For instance, a young minister had a disappointment recently and seemed downcast over it. I said to him, "Are you discouraged?" He hesitated a moment, which made me to know that he was. I said, "Do you believe that all things work together for good to them that love the Lord, to them that are called according to His purpose?"[14] His answer was "Yes." I said, "Then you ought to rejoice in that all things do work together for good on your behalf."

Now we begin to get into some of the ways and means of offsetting unbelief. You remember, at the first of this discourse, we can reply

(11)    Security of the Believer - Dr. Guy Duffield
(12)    Hebrews 6:4-6
(13)    Nehemiah 8:10
(14)    Romans 8:28

with the man who when the Lord asked, "Do you believe," answered, "Lord I believe. Help thou mine unbelief." In other words, he admitted the presence of unbelief. I think this is good. I think this is proper. I think we should confess our unbelief *to the Lord.* Not continually, and to others. Confess it to the Lord, ask Him to forgive you and to help you to do something about it. I genuinely feel, by the help of the Lord, that I have found what I shall call, "A Sure Cure for Unbelief" and I would like to share it with you here.

"If thou hast thought evil, lay thy hand upon thine mouth."

I like that! This is how I can stop the evils of unbelief. I can't stop them from coming to my mind. If I wake up in the morning with the symptoms of sickness, it is there and I can't stop my mind from recognizing it. I can't train my mind well enough to ignore the pain impulses my body sends to my brain.

It is impossible to keep these things from entering your mind . . . these thoughts, evil thoughts of unbelief. What are we to do when we have these evil thoughts of unbelief? *Lay thy hand upon thy mouth!* Here is the sure cure for unbelief. *Don't speak it!* This will keep unbelief from laying hold of you. Lay your hand upon your mouth! Don't speak the thoughts of unbelief. *Don't magnify your unbelief... magnify your faith. This positive faith will preempt unbelief!*

(15)     Proverbs 30:32

47

# CHAPTER 10

# FAITH, THE PATHFINDER

James 5:11 says: "Ye have heard of the patience of Job."

I wish that this was all that we had heard about this wonderful man and his faith and patience. This chronicle has been used for a crutch. Used as a crutch, down through the ages, by thousands of suffering people who have compared themselves and their experiences to Job. They have used him as an example of "the righteous who suffer." They have used him as an excuse many times. They have said, "Job suffered so he would learn patience, maybe I can learn also."

Before we can justifiably use Job as an excuse for the neglect of our faith or before we can use this great man of God as an example of the reason the Lord permits the enemy to torment and afflict us . . . it will be wise to examine what the Bible teaches and what really happened.

First of all, let us be very careful in using the story of Job as an example of all the saints. God did not use him as an example of all saints. *God used him as a singular, express example of the degree of righteousness that a mortal man can attain.* God did not use Job as an example of the average saint. We could wish this were true. He used him as an example of a saint that was above and beyond all saints that ever lived in the earth. The Scripture states that there was not another like him in the earth.[1] We do well to remember this if we endeavour to compare ourselves with Job.

Secondly, let us notice that Job is not an example of how promiscuously God permits Satan to have access to diabolically harass his people. Notice that the challenge of Satan to God is, in effect, "I know more than you know about your own people . . . I am a better judge of human nature than you. I know something that you do not. I know Job better than you do even though you say he is the epitome of all saints."

God does not let the hedge down for Satan to have liberty with his saints, to prove the saints. This is not an example of "trying a saint" for the good of the saint. *It is an example of the conflict between God*

(1)    Job 1:8

48

*and Satan . . . and man is caught in the middle! It is the battle of the eternal ages continued!* Even though Satan failed in his bid to overcome God . . . he has not always failed in his bid for God's people, whom God loves. This is proven by Satan's attack against Adam and Eve in the Garden of Eden. What Satan is literally saying is, "God, once and for all, I am going to prove to you that I know more than you know. You say you know Job . . . I am going to prove to you that you don't know as much as you think you know!" Satan is not only the false accuser of the brethren, but the book of Job teaches that he is the false accuser of God himself!

Why, then, did God take the hedge down? To prove to us all, and to all in the eternities, that God is God! God omnipotent! God omniscient! God immutable! *When God makes a statement concerning the righteousness of one or all of his saints, it cannot be successfully challenged.* It will withstand all tests.

In the third place, let us talk about another misunderstanding that people are prone to have about Job. They say, "Look what great gains he made!" This is true in the material sense. He received twice as much as he had in the beginning. However, we must remember that God declared Job to be perfect(2) in His sight to begin with. This perfection is absolute, it cannot be improved. It is very interesting, inasmuch as we are dealing partially in this book about wrong speaking, that Job's repentance in Chapter 42 deals with his thoughtless speaking. Notice this especially in verse three.

> "I thoughtlessly confused the issues. I spoke without intellignece of wonders far beyond my ken."(3)

This wonderful miraculous faith we have is a constant pathfinder through every difficulty. It is the faith that will take you through. This is not the faith one gets by suffering and torment. Where did Job get his triumphant faith that saw him through his extreme testing? Did he get it because he suffered? Did he get it after he went through so many losses? Did his faith increase day after day because he languished in suffering? No, a thousand times no! *The faith that Job had, that did take him through, was the faith that he had when he started! This is the faith that will see you through every trial you have! This is the faith given to us by the Lord.*

Don't wish for the trials and tests of Job to make you stronger. Don't accept the troubles that Satan will bring to your door because

(2)   Job 1:8
(3)   Moffatt

49

you want to be another Job. *There was only one Job.* God's appraisal of him was correct. He was an outstanding saint. He had what God knew he had . . . the faith that would see him through. Faith, the pathfinder! Through every trial, difficulty, and test!

Through God we shall do valiantly!

"Greater is He that is in you, than He that is in the world."(4)

Cherish your faith. Confess your faith. Constantly confirm your faith by your actions.

There is no doubt that the kind of trials through which Job's faith took him cannot be entered into and one emerge victoriously but what the person's faith will be much stronger. All of life's experiences, trials, and tests cannot be endured without great recompense of reward. *But this enduring faith, the answer to all generations, is a glorious faith that we have, given to us by the Lord, that will find a path through all the entanglements that result by the challenges of Satan.*

Another great and valuable lesson from the kind of trials and tests that confront us, such as Job's testing, is to be learned from those who surrounded Job during his ordeal. Job received no help from his immediate loved ones. There is a reason for this. A loved one is usually emotionally involved. Job's wife was thus when she observed the constant, incessant suffering of one she dearly loved. Usually the first reaction of a loved one is to put an immediate end to suffering via the first means available. If your loved one goes through a similar suffering, the kind of assistance they need is the kind that comes through your faith ... rather than your deeply felt sympathy. Sympathy is usually the result of being emotionally involved. Compassion is a result of the entering into, as Jesus did, when he had compassion on the multitudes. Compassion "bears" whereas sympathy is "merely extended."

Much is to be learned also, when one endures trials of faith, from so called "Job's comforter." We need each other at all times. Much more during trials of our faith. The poor example of Job's comforters can teach us a lesson in how to be good comforters. Their beginning was good. They sat in silence and comforted by their presence. It was only when they spoke out in judgment that they ceased to minister comfort.

Let us rally around a brother or a sister during his time of trial. This wonderful visible faith is not only comfort, but is also a faith that will see us through to victory.

(4)   1 John 4:4        50

# CHAPTER 11

# FAITH THAT PROTECTS

Who is the Spirit filled believer? First let us notice that he is a believer. He, the Spirit filled believer, gives credence to all that the other fundamental believers do, concerning the scripture and eternal verities cherished down through the ages. However, the Charismatic believer is more than just a believer. He is a Spirit filled believer. This means he is partaker of the same experience that the 120 followers of Christ received in the upper room on the day of Pentecost, as related in the second chapter of Acts. This experience is a tremendous spiritual victory. *The believer has dared to enter into an experience, by faith, that is greatly rewarding.* However glorious this experience is, it also has some attendant stigmas that go with it. Not all believers will rejoice with you when you relate to them that you are baptized in the Spirit. Some rather think that you are just emotional, others that you are unstable and perhaps even a little "touched in the head."

Thank God for the Spirit filled believer who knows what he has in Christ, and in the power of the Holy Spirit, and is very happy and contented to suffer any reproach that may come his way. If we are going to suffer some reproach in this experience, let us by all means get all that is coming to us as *promised by the scriptures.* Let us endeavour to walk in all the promises that He has given unto us. We are different and we do have more than others who have not this experience. We are very bold to declare this and, from the scripture, we can verify it. However, sad to say, we have not always exemplified this added touch of the Spirit by our practices.

*Here, I desire to speak of walking in all of the finished work of the cross.* This means all of the benefits of salvation, the baptism of the blessed Holy Spirit, and Divine Healing, and the glorious hope of the soon return of our Lord. Let us examine a great portion of scripture found in the book of Matthew 16:19. Inasmuch as other writers, great writers, have proven conclusively that Christ gave the keys of the kingdom to the church and not to the person of Peter, we will not take the time to again go into a duplication. Suffice to say that the Lord Jesus did give his keys of the kingdom of heaven to his followers. If he gave them to us, then we have them. It is important then to notice the great and tremendous power that accompanies these keys.

The Lord Jesus says that "whatever you bind on earth will be bound in heaven." I like Moffatt's translation of this which states, "whatever you prohibit on earth will be prohibited in heaven." One can also use the word "stop" and be in complete accord with the translation of this verse. If this verse of scripture is true, and certainly we believe the Word, then we will have to concur that what God is saying here is, "I will only prohibit up here what you prohibit down there." Further, in this same translation, "Whatever you permit on earth, will be permitted in heaven." E.V. Rieu's translation uses the word "allow." God, again, is saying, "I will allow in heaven, only what you will allow down there." Exploration of this verse will explain why many premature deaths occur. It will explain the incidence of many untimely accidents. God, in His great love, often has tried to warn us of impending danger by speaking to us in dreams, premonitions of danger, and visions. We have not been taught the right reaction to these warnings. If God has chosen to stop in heaven what we stop on this earth, then this explains many things that have been hard for Christians to understand down through the years.

Some time ago, I was preaching on the subject of "Clearing GOD'S Name" and proclaiming His great love and concern for us. A man was present who had gone to church for fifteen years but had never given his heart to Christ. Upon hearing that it was our fault, and not God's, that we Christians have these calamitous experiences, he gave his heart to the Lord at the conclusion of the service. This cleared up something that had bothered him for years. No, Christian, it is not God's fault, it is very often ours. I knew of a young pentecostal preacher whom God had given, through dreams and premonitions, warning of impending death by accident. He, not having learned or been taught this great truth, allowed fear to come into his heart. He accepted the warning as a warning of something that was inevitable. He died in an accident soon after. The church was deprived of a talented ministry. Children were deprived of a father and the young wife became a widow. Was this God's will? I, for one, cannot blame God for this . . . and find myself at variance with any doctrine that would dare place responsibility upon God for such action.

A pastor recently told me of an automobile accident that came very close to taking his life. He was travelling the legal speed limit of seventy miles an hour and lost control of the car. The car rolled over many times. Only the grace of God and the pastor's presence of mind in quickly moving to the middle of the seat and grasping the seat frame with his hands saved him from serious injury and possible death. I asked him if he had had a warning, and he said that he had and also his wife had this same premonition of danger. What are we to do in these circumstances? God does not warn us because death, accident, injury, etc., is inevitable. God warns us so that we may *take authority against it.* I had such a warning the other day. I took authority over it in the Name of Jesus and claimed protection. I was driving and, just one short block from where I had the premonition and had taken authority over it, I was saved from a very serious accident and there was no skill of mine involved. When God shows you, as His child, that something is going to happen to you or a loved one, take these simple steps. *Thank the Lord for showing you the danger, bind it, take authority over it stopping it in the name of Jesus, and it will be stopped in heaven.*

Just briefly to touch on Divine Healing. Many times we do not allow the healing of Christ to flow to us because we do not permit it. Rather, we claim the sickness, even stating it is the will of God for us to suffer. Thus God is blamed for allowing his children to go through trying times. He does not desire this. He, in His great love, laid our infirmities on Christ that we would not have to suffer these infirmities and diseases.

Not only from sickness and accidents have I found this great truth to be highly effective, but in all of the work of the Lord. I recall an experience we had, while pastoring, that illustrates the effectiveness of this great truth in an area other than sickness or accident. This was an occasion that involved a serious breach between two of our most faithful families. This, if allowed to continue, would have an adverse effect on the whole church. This is the work of the enemy. I didn't call the involved parties in and try to straighten out the situation by counselling. This is sometimes the proper course of action. This time my wife and I went to prayer. We bound the enemy and demanded that he stop in his operation against the unity of the church. We claim this promise that, if we stopped it down here, the Lord would stop it in heaven. This happened on a Sunday morning. In a matter of a few hours the breach was healed and all was well.

*I am satisfied that many church quarrels and splits could have been healed if the servants of the Lord had taken these steps in stopping it.* I enjoyed the testimony of Rev. Charles Hollis at one of our recent conventions. The Lord had awakened his wife in the middle of the night and given her this verse and this enabled them to deal effectively with what had been a very sticky problem. As a pastor many years I have had some of my finest members suddenly, and for some unexplainable reason, become angry with me. I thank God for the many times we have stopped the enemy from working in their lives and making all well in just the matter of a few days . . . with never a word having been spoken between us. Just the Lord stopping in heaven what we had stopped in earth.(1)

This great truth, the victory that comes to us because of Christ giving the keys of the kingdom to his people, has worked for many people in a different way. The principle is always the same. Years ago we experienced a great miracle in our home. When our second son was born, the doctor informed us that he had a spastic condition from the waist down, and, if he lived, would not walk. When the doctor told me this I recall answering him, "But doctor, we believe in prayer." He answered that we had better pray then. As far as I know, there is no known medical cure for a spastic condition, but God undertook in a marvelous way and our son lived and has enjoyed a normal, healthy life.

Pastors, future pastors, lay workers in the harvest field of the Lord, act upon this great doctrine! Don't talk negatively about problems and wonder what you are going to do about them. Don't talk defeat and accept discouragement. *Stop! Bind! Prohibit* these things and God will *Stop, Bind and Prohibit* them in heaven. Don't permit the enemy to defeat you. If you permit it down here . . . God must permit it in heaven! Permit only the good things of God to come your way. The negatives of life will come. There will be battles, physically, materially, and mentally . . . but, thank God, He will see us through because He has already paid the price. He purchased our victory and we will not be defeated because *we have the victory.*

(1)     26 Translations, Page 68

# CHAPTER 12

# FAITH THAT PARALYZES FEAR

All mortals will agree with 1 John 4:18 when it states that *fear hath torment. Perhaps, at one time or another, in all of our lives, we have experienced times of tormenting fear. Let us be sure, in the very beginning, that we recognize the scriptural admonitions to fear God. I rather like W.E. Vine's way of putting it, "A wholesome dread of displeasing God."*[1] We agree with this. It is a different type of fear than the fear that causes torment, distinct from the fear that is a robber of our faith. What is this force that can cause paralyzing fear? A force that can so bind a person with fear that they cannot be effective for God. Our missionaries from New Guinea tell us that there is such fear of the witch doctor that, when he pronounces a curse, fear of such great magnitude grips the victim that it oftentimes causes death.[2] Even here in our North American society we see many gripped by fear. Acrophobia, the fear of lightning . . . these, and many other fears and phobias haunt us. Fear not only has torment, but it is a great robber of our faith. *When fear comes in the mind, faith goes out of the heart.*

The disciples were rebuked by the Lord Jesus:[3]

> "And he said unto them, Why are ye so fearful? How is it that ye have no faith?"

Moffatt's translation:

> "How little you trust God."

In this incident of the Lord stilling the storm, we find typical followers of the Lord Jesus. They had trust and confidence until conditions became menacing. Then fear came in and faith left. Did the Lord Jesus sympathize with them in their fear? No! He gave them stern rebuke. Is it amazing to us that the Lord had this attitude toward fear on this occasion? Let us examine the word as it is used in this instance. This same word, "fearful," is found only in three

(1)    N.T. Words, Page 84
(2)    Reverend Mason Hughes
(3)    Mark 4:40

55

places in the New Testament. It heads the list found in Revelation 21:8 of those who have their part in the Lake of Fire along with those guilty of such terrible sins as unbelief, murder, whoremongering, lying, and all that which is abominable. Every instance in which this word is used is always connected with that which is the direct opposite of faith.

Superstitions, heard as a child, can follow us through our entire lives. The writer, even to this day, cannot eat a piece of fish and drink milk together without an involuntary twinge of warning. Why? Because, as a small lad, I can recall hearing, "If you eat fish and drink milk, you will die." Perhaps the black cat crossing the path or the Friday the 13th still sends a shiver up the spine! Many adults o this day fear a dark room. But the fearfulness that Jesus rebuked here is a *fear that drives out faith.* It is the opposite of a faith that is firmly fixed on the Word of God.

The Bible declares that whom the Son sets free is free indeed.(4) We are to be free from the fears that would bind us. Many good potential gospel workers are not in the ministry today because they could not overcome their fears. Even some of those who prepared themselves and went out into the ministry would be there today if they could have overcome their fears. They say, "I am afraid to do this . . . or that." Let the words of the scripture burn their way deeply into your soul . . . even into the subconscious realm. *For God hath not given us the spirit of fear but of power and of love, and of a sound mind.*(5) Any time there is the slightest essence of fear, it does not come from God. Let us not repeat the fears that come our way, and it is inevitable that they will come. Let us not repeat those negative things which do not come from the Lord. On the other hand, let us not lie and be untruthful. Perhaps there are some fears that continue to follow us about. To overcome this, let us go our way *speaking the word of God,* the great promises of God. These shall dominate our fears. It is a scriptural admonition of *"fear not, believe only."*(6)

I have known of people who exercised faith for the healing of their bodies. They were experiencing victory until, hearing about someone who died having the same affliciton, fear came in and faith left.

You may recall the time when Jesus was on his way to the house of Jairus, to heal his sick daughter. Word came that Jairus was not to

(4)    John 8:36
(5)    2 Timothy 1:7
(6)    Luke 8:50

56

trouble the Master any longer because his daughter had died. Quickly Jesus said, "Be not afraid, only believe." What He said in effect was, "Don't let what you have just heard bring fear into your heart; keep on believing." Jesus knew that fear could overcome faith . . . *He also knew faith could overcome fear!* I have known of students who, upon graduation from Bible College, received their appointment and with great faith and anticipation in their hearts set out to fulfill their divine calling. Alas, on the way they met some of Job's comforters . . . "Where did you say you were going? Oh, I feel sorry for you . . . that place is a preacher-killer!" Ultimately, their ears are so filled with negatives that the old nemesis of fear begins to rear its ugly head and, if they are not careful, faith will leave as fear comes in.

One may well assume that there are two types of believers. Two verses in Psalms differentiate between them. One verse says, "What time I am afraid, I will trust in the Thee." This type of individual, when fear does come in, will trust the Lord. This is good, but there is something better. "I will trust in the Lord and *not be afraid.*" The former verse covers the majority of saints; the latter, the minority. Very few people have come to the place where their trust in God has produced an utter fearlessness. Few say, "I will trust in the Lord and refuse to be afraid; I will not let fear dominate me." Perhaps one of the reasons we have so many small churches is because of a fear of stepping out in faith to attempt something big for God. All great men of God took great risks in their fearlessness. It is regrettable that, many times, the keen, sharp enthusiasm of a pastor to launch a vigorous new program has been dulled by a member who said, "We tried that and it won't work here." It is true that we can have human failures along many lines, *but let us not become bound by the fear of another's failure.*

I recently talked with a worker who had to drop out of the ministry because of sickness. She confessed that she had completely recovered; but said that if she and her husband entered the ministry again she *feared* the same thing would occur. Thus the Kingdom of God is robbed of badly needed and capable workers who are haunted by the fear of a former difficulty. Dr. McMillan, in his book, None of These Diseases, states "Sleep will rest us from physical fatigue, but not from worry." *Worry and fear are first cousins.* This may be the reason why many people are so tired in the morning . . . just as tired as they were when they went to bed.

57

Let us remember to speak our faith often.

"For God hath hot given us the spirit of fear, but of power and of love, and of a sound mind."(7)

Many good Christians will take their God given faith and believe the wrong things. Recently a person came to me and said, "I just can't believe that God loves me or hears me." I said, "Do you believe in and have you received Him?" The answer was, "Yes, but I have no feeling or knowledge He has accepted me." I asked him if he would begin to swear and use His name in vain. The answer was, "No, I believe He would hear me." Then I said take that same faith and believe He now hears you as you tell Him you love Him. He did and a big smile came on his face.

This wonderful heritage, this great God-given faith, has the answer to every generation's frustrations, worries, and fears. But it has to be believed, confessed and acted upon and when done will bring peace and victories.

(7)    2 Timothy 1:7

# CHAPTER 13

# FAITH AND THE PATRIARCHS

I suppose if one were to examine the Bible in its entirety and try to find some individual therein that would best illustrate faith, there would be numerous examples from which to choose. It does seem, however, that there was one such man, the father of us all, who is a striking esample of the subject with which we will now deal. His name was Abram. You will say, "Dr. Hicks, you have made a mistake . . . his name was Abraham." No, his name was Abram originally. Then, one day, God made him a promise and changed his name to Abraham.[1] After that, every time he was called "Abraham" undoubtedly it reminded him of the promise of God.

You will remember that this was an aged man, far past the vigor of his youth, and God promised him that there would come from his loins a son. In Romans 4 we read about this. Here was a great man . . . the father of the Jewish nation and, therefore, earthly father of all christian people. In Romans 4 it speaks of Abraham as "against hope believing in hope." In other words, when all hope in the natural was gone, *his faith caused him to keep on believing.* He had nothing else to hope for or believe in, except his faith . . . that he might become the father of many nations according to that which was spoken, "So shall thy seed be . . ."

This same Abraham, his body now dead, had nothing in which to hope. The body of his wife Sarah no longer had the ability to produce life because of her age and the "deadness of her womb." The Bible says, though he had nothing to hope in, "Abraham hoped on in faith." *His faith in God's word gave him hope.* One version states "Who, in hope, believed against hope."[2] In other words, his faith was stronger than his hopelessness when he looked at his own body and the deadness of Sarah's womb. Romans 4:19 says:

"And being not weak in faith, he considered not his own body now dead."

*He gave no heed to the symptoms of age,* nor the hopeless conditions.

(1)    Genesis 17:5
(2)    Romans 4:17 (A.R.V.)

He was not ruled by what he saw with his eyes. He did not believe what his sense of feeling said to him. Verse 20 says "he staggered not." He staggered not at the prevailing, hopeless situation that his eyes saw. He did not waver; he did not give in.

When you begin to look at what your senses will tell you, what you feel, what you see, what you hear . . . unbelief will come in! It will stagger you and cause you to waver in unbelief. *Abraham never once staggered.*(3) Have you visited a rest home? As a pastor, I visited the old peoples' homes many times. I visited the city hospitals of cities where we have pastored churches. It always seemed to me that there were so very many of the old and poor there, people who were very old, lying there day after day, nothing but skin and bones. Many times their eyes were bright and you were aware that their intelligence far surpassed their physical condition . . . but their bodies were at the point of death. Memories of these visits more forcefully impress me of the bold, daring faith of Abraham and Sarah.

Please keep in mind that he was one hundred years old.(4) Picture these two, a one hundred year old white haired man and his ninety year old wife, saying, in audacious faith, "We are going to have a child." The first reaction of those listening would be to say, "You are crazy." As a matter of fact, in this day, if anyone talks like that, we have places where we put them!

As time passes . . . Abraham is still holding to his confession . . . still looking forward to holding his own son in his arms. He should know better than this! Unto what then is he clinging? He would answer, "I am holding on to God's promise. I am believing against hope, and all hopelessness, because God gave me this promise and I believe God." He staggered not, he wavered not, he was undaunted! He kept right on believing. He staggered not at the promise of God through unbelief, but he was strong in the faith. How? *By giving glory to God!*(5) His confession was that being fully persuaded that what God had promised He was able to perform. He was giving voice to the fact that he believed God every day for a son. He is the father of faith. He believed what God had said. "Well, Abraham, it is testimony time. What is your testimony?" "I want to stand and thank God for a son. I want to praise Him for giving me a son that will be my heir. I am going to have generation after generation . . . multitudes that cannot be numbered, even as the sands of the sea cannot be numbered."

(3)    Romans 4:20
(4)    Romans 4:19
(5)    Romans 4:20

The question would probably be on many minds of the people who would hear this testimony, "How can this be possible?" This seems to be the concern of a lot of people. "I wonder how God can work it out?" "I wonder how God can do it?" You let it alone. This is God's business. Ours is to be strong and dare to believe God unwaveringly. Use your imagination with me a little bit. On a certain morning, as Sarah and Abraham sat at breakfast, Abraham looked across the table and saw a light and color in Sarah's countenance that had not been there before. He sensed the evidence of the answer to his faith. Oh! You say, that must have made him shout! No, he had been shouting for years. He had been steadily believing for years. But it still must have been a wonderful day when God began to bring to pass in this couple's elderly bodies the promise that He had made so many years ago.

This faith we have, given to us of God, is our most priceless possession. It hurts me, literally hurts me, to hear good Christian people say, "I don't have much faith." God gave them faith. The Bible says He hath dealt to every man the measure of faith.[6] Faith cometh by hearing, and hearing by the Word.[7] They are going by their five senses and not giving proper place to that wonderful God-given sixth sense, their faith.

I know of a lady who asked prayer to be healed of cancer. It was a skin cancer on her face. She was taught to give praise and glory to God, as Abraham did. She praised the Lord that her cancer was healed. Well, people being as they are, talked. They said, "Anyone can see that her cancer is still there." In fact, her husband chided her about it. She said, "I am going to continue praising the Lord." Several months went by and she was still believing and testifying of her healing. People would nudge each other and her husband was embarrassed to hear her claims. One day she was in the bedroom and looked in the mirror. She put her hand up to her face and something came off in her hand. It was the unsightly cancer. She began to praise the Lord and her husband thought, "Oh no, she's at it again." She said, "It's gone. Come and see."

I have heard good men say that we should not claim a thing before we have it. They say to do this is improper. Perhaps they should read the account of Abraham again. I heard one of the best evangelists of our day (this is not hearsay, I heard him) say that he did not believe

(6)    Romans 12:3
(7)    Romans 10:17

in this nonsense about claiming your healing before you received it. I suppose if Abraham had attended on one of his meetings and arose to testify being one hundred years old, "I want to thank God for giving me a son," there would have been someone dispatched to quiet this aged man and his testimony. Someone to tell him, "Hush, old man, you are not to claim a thing before you receive it!" I like to put it this way *claim something before it is done and rejoice over it before it is done, and you are acting your faith.* This is what Abraham did. He was strong in giving praise to God when there was no evidence that he had any right to give God praise. Yet he was strong in faith, giving glory to God. Paraphrased Epistles puts it this way, "He praised God for the blessing before it ever happened."(8)

Years ago, as a young minister, I needed an automobile. As I was praying about this one day, I felt a witness in my heart. I began to rejoice as though I was already driving down the street in this car. A few weeks later, when this became a reality, I wondered why I wasn't more excited? Why I didn't have a greater feeling of exuberance as I drove along? Then I remembered. I had really rejoiced several weeks before, when I was in prayer!

Abraham believed God when all hope was gone. He praised God above all circumstances, and thus received from God. The pentecostal believers' faith, the faith that is the answer to all generations was pioneered many generations ago by Abraham, the father of faith. Many of our own successful, present day ministers are following in the steps of the patriarchs. One such pastor states, "There is no believing but what climaxes in confession." Believing and confession are very closely related. God's Word is the standard of our life with the result that the level of our life will rise to the level of our confession of the Word.(9)

(8)    Romans 4:20 Paraphrased Epistles
(9)    Reverend Victor Gardner

# CHAPTER 14

# FAITH AND PITFALLS

If all clergymen were gathered together and asked to compile a list of pitfalls of which to be beware, a long, long list would result. Perhaps all of them have been experienced. The ones stipulated as heading the list would be long debated. Let us begin by using one most familiar.

After many years of experience, and having had to deal with it in my own heart, I have come to the personal conclusion that, in my opinion, *pride* would have to head the list. Another reason for its priority is because it is first in God's catalogue in Proverbs 1:6-17. This alone should cause us to give careful study to the reason why pride heads the list . . . because everything we have received is from the Lord! All spiritual progress is the result of the great unmerited favor and grace of God.

It is no wonder that God despises pride when it shows up in our life, as though we have as a result of our own doing something for which we should be proud or boastful. We will not here go into all the scriptures that deal with this sin.[1] Just the fact that it is a sin will cause us to know that our faith cannot work for us if this hindrance is there.[2]

There are very few people whom God can trust with success. They immediately begin to think that because God has blessed their work, they are then entitled to criticize others. They become convinced that because they have been successful in getting answers to their prayers, it must be that they have a closer relationship to God than others; they then have become a favorite with God and can do no wrong! Thus, in reality, they set up a little kingdom and begin to build *for* themselves and *around* themselves. Satan has taken advantage of this pitfall to ruin many effective gospel workers and even laymen.

Saints sometime think of themselves more highly than they ought, even superior to their pastor because they have experienced great

(1)    Proverbs 29:23
(2)    Psalms 66:18

63

answers to their prayers. Can God trust you with success? Can He give you the answers to your prayers that you so greatly desire? If he does, can you walk humbly before Him? I have frequently told our ministers that, when the time comes when God can bless them and answer their prayers so they will have great growth when they attend a convention genuinely hoping that they are *not* called upon to relate their success and great knowledge then will they be found relatively free from pride and be found walking in true humility.

Another great pitfall to faith is *over-extending* the faith that you have. I once counselled with a gospel worker who, with her husband, greatly desired to quit their jobs, and to fully trust the Lord for their complete sustenance. Their example reminded me of the time that Peter was in the same boat! You will recall that Peter greatly over-extended his faith when he desired to walk on the water. People are guilty of wanting to do that thing that will make them stand out from the others . . . "Hey, look at me! I can walk on the water!" The Lord is pictured as always encouraging our faith.[3] We must be the ones that are responsible to see that we do not over-extend this wonderful faith that God has given unto us. These same aforementioned gospel workers were desirous of doing a noble deed but, under the circumstances that confronted them, they were *over-extending* their faith. They had already incurred so much debt that the amount they needed to be free from secular work called for more faith than they had ever exercised, at least up to this occasion.

I am not one to believe that we should encourage a person to attempt a great feat that involves the supernatural before he is ready. Perhaps some of the healing evangelists (so called) err along this line when they encourage some very desperately sick people to lay aside their medicine and trust the Lord completely. I agree with the Quakers. When someone asked them when he should lay aside his sword, the answer was "When thou canst." It is not the responsibility of one to tell another to lay aside his medicine or to quit his job. These great decisions involving one's faith and God must be made by the person involved and not an outsider.

Another pitfall to be avoided is the *lack of encouragement* one receives from other people. Usually we receive negative advice. Can't you use your imagination and hear what the other disciples were saying to Peter: "Watch out Peter, you will drown." "How do

(3)    Matthew 14:29
(4)    1 Samuel 30:6

you know it is the Lord?" "Boy, I wouldn't do that for a million dollars." "You had better think twice, Peter." Perhaps the time that the men spoke of stoning David is a good illustration of what to do when those around you fail to encourage you, that is, David encouraged himself in the Lord His God.(4)

Not only pride and over-extending our faith; but faith exercised under great emotional distress or in the time of fear is seldom effective. Not only is Peter's attempt to walk on the water an example of this, but also the time that the children of Israel failed at the entrance to Canaan land. They were greatly distressed because they had failed to believe the positive report of the two spies, but rather chose to believe the ten spies, that caused them to miss the will of God. They then attempted, under great emotional stress, to go against the enemies, which ended in disaster.(5)

Too many of God's children wait to exercise faith when trouble comes, usually in time of emotional upheaval. It is better not to wait until it is greatly, urgently needed to try to exercise faith. It is better to exercise faith every day. This is why a Spirit filled child of God should pray in the Spirit daily. Even time we pray with the Spirit, we exercise great faith because we "by-pass" our minds and improve ourselves.(6) Also, one should daily read the scripture because faith cometh by hearing and hearing by the Word of God.(7)

One of the greatest failures of the faith principles to work successfully is the lack of forgiveness in the seekers heart. Mark 11:23-24 is followed by our Lord Jesus admonition to forgive. Many are unaware of harbored feelings or have even forgotten resentments. If the answer to your petition isn't forthcoming, search your heart and be sure you aren't holding something against someone, because if you haven't forgiven all, your Father can't forgive you and thus your request can't be given, your confession of faith for your desire denied.

May we conclude this chapter on pitfalls by identifying the architect of these evilly designed traps. Satan himself is the evil one. He is the usurper, joykiller, home wrecker, the rapist of the body, afflicter, pain giver. He plays skillfully upon high strung nerves, then tortures, terrifies, tears and tempts. He paints glowing pictures of satisfying lust over the human canvas of destroying social diseases. He prospers the wicked, propels delusions, propagates lies,

(5)   Numbers 14:40-45
(6)   Jude 20
(7)   Romans 10:17

65

petuates slavery. He involves millions and then enslaves them. He encourages disobedience, engulfs backsliders, introduces half-truths, invites destruction. He removes the gospel seed and plants thorns. He encourages worldliness and destroys holiness by discouragement. He is the beginning of every destructive criticism, the author of petty fault finding, the architect of suffering, the arranger of evil and the executor at death. He is the pilot of every airplane whose passengers are made up of overthrown preachers, backslidden evangelists and lukewarm church members, and ex-Sunday School teachers, and gospel workers.

*Our great example, our pattern is always the Lord Jesus Christ, if we are to successfully avoid the many pitfalls that will endanger our great expectations.*

# CHAPTER 15

# FAITH AND PERFECTION

The subject which we will now consider will make a fitting climax. It is the believers' supreme object. When our faith is working for us, in us, and through us, it should be faith that worketh by *love*.(1)

In the thirteenth chapter of First Corinthians we have this wonderful ultimate goal of every Christian clearly spelled out in understandable terms. If, after even a simple perusal of these verses, one could be satisfied without love, their lives would certainly continue on with a hollow sound. Whenever we speak of the believers' love we must not forget that the Word declares God is Love.(2) If God is love, His children, being born of God, should possess all of the characteristics of their Heavenly Father, love being paramount.

And now abideth faith, hope, charity (love), these three; but the greatest of these is *love*.(3) Notice that this trinity of great attributes is begun by the mentioning of *faith*. This is as it should be, for faith is primarily essential and has to do with our relationship to God our Heavenly Father. It is by faith that one reaches out into the spiritual realm. It is this same wonderful faith whereby one is saved. Faith is not being minimized in this order of continuity. It is neither mentioned as being greater than love, and this is as it should be. Faith is the beginning and, as it is exercised, it leads to the next in order which is hope.

Hope is not faith. Many people have made the great mistake of beginning with hope, trusting that it will produce results for them. No doubt all of us have heard someone remark in relation to receiving something from God, "I surely hope so." Some have even been heard to remark, 'I'm just a 'prayin' and a 'hopin'.'" *Faith produces hope* . . . not vice versa. This leads us to the great verse that teaches us, because of hope, the Love of God is shed abroad in our hearts by the Holy Ghost.(4) When one has faith, he will also have hope. Hope makes us positive. Hope keeps us out of the negative realm. When

(1)    Galations 5:6b
(2)    1 John 4:8b
(3)    1 Corinthians 13:13
(4)    Romans 5:5

you meet someone who seems to be discouraged and you ask him if he believes God, he may answer in the affirmative but it is painfully obvious that he has lost hope. If faith is given to us by God then, assuredly, we can express the hope that faith produces. Perhaps this is an area that we can bring more into a practical realm by expressing our hope more vociferously. *Hope, therefore, becomes an attitude.* Hope, therefore, becomes a way of life. The Bible refers us to the great hope that became part of Abraham's life.[5] We should always express the hope that faith has given to us rather than expressing the difficulties that surround us. Far too many believers have yet to learn to express their hopes at times other than just prayer meeting time when testimonies are being received. Have you expressed you hope today? When you arise each morning to meet a new day, why not begin that day by expressing your hope! When you sense the menacing approach of trouble and difficulties, sing out loudly of your hope that is born of faith and trust in your Heavenly Father.

But the greatest of these is Love. Is there a mistake here? Is Love the greatest? If the Scripture so states, then it is true. But we have failed, by practice, to corroborate this. The visible kingdom of God in this earth has a history of church quarrels and divisions . . . when it should have been known for its love.[6] This is characteristic of God. We are, rather, known by the characteristics of man. Love, the Love of God, is not natural; it is supernatural. If God so loved us we ought also to love one another.[7] This is to be our practice. Love covers a multitude of sins.[8] Notice that it does not "uncover." Far too many Christians "uncover" sins by talking about them. Perhaps one of our greater sins is to uncover sins that have been already covered by the blood of Jesus. The next time you hear of someone's sins, do not discuss them or the person involved; rather pray for them, thus revealing your love for them to your Heavenly Father.

Love is the greatest of these because of the three mentioned Love alone is eternal. When we go into the eternities we will no longer need either faith or hope. Love should become our chief goal. It is eternal. It is of God. Let it become a greater part of your daily life. Practice it. Pursue it until its riches permeate your attitude. What a glorious day that will be when the Christians' faith becomes perfected in Love.

(5)    Romans 4:18
(6)    John 13:35
(7)    1 John 4:11
(8)    1 Peter 4:8b